BASIC ITALIAN:
A GRAMMAR AND WORKBOOK

Basic Italian: A Grammar and Workbook comprises an accessible reference grammar and related exercises in a single volume.

This workbook presents 23 individual grammar points in lively and realistic contexts. Each unit consists of jargon-free explanations and comparisons with English, targeting the more common difficulties experienced by learners of Italian. Grammar points are followed by examples and exercises selected to make use of contemporary Italian.

Basic Italian introduces Italian culture and people through the medium of the language used today, providing readers with the basic tools to express themselves in a wide variety of situations.

Features include:

- examples in both Italian and English

- grammar tables for easy reference

- full exercise answer key

- glossary of grammatical terms

Basic Italian is the ideal reference and practice book for beginners and also for students with some knowledge of the language.

Stella Peyronel is a lecturer at the University of Turin, Italy. She has taught Italian to foreigners for over 20 years and is the author of several Italian grammars. **Ian Higgins** is Honorary Senior Lecturer at the University of St Andrews and is co-author of *Thinking Italian Translation*.

Other titles available in the *Grammar Workbooks* series are:

Basic Cantonese
Intermediate Cantonese

Basic Chinese
Intermediate Chinese

Basic German
Intermediate German

Basic Polish
Intermediate Polish

Basic Russian
Intermediate Russian

Basic Welsh
Intermediate Welsh

Titles of related interest published by Routledge:

Colloquial Italian, Second Edition
by Sylvia Lymbery

Modern Italian Grammar: A Practical Guide, Second Edition
by Anna Proudfoot and Francesco Cardo

Modern Italian Grammar Workbook, Second Edition
by Anna Proudfoot

BASIC ITALIAN:
A GRAMMAR AND
WORKBOOK

Stella Peyronel and Ian Higgins

Routledge
Taylor & Francis Group

LONDON AND NEW YORK

First published 2006
by Routledge
2 Park Square, Milton Park, Abingdon OX14 4RN, UK

Simultaneously published in the USA and Canada
by Routledge
270 Madison Ave, New York, NY 10016

Routledge is an imprint of the Taylor & Francis Group

© 2006 Stella Peyronel and Ian Higgins

Typeset in Times by RefineCatch Limited, Bungay, Suffolk
Printed and bound in Great Britain by MPG Books Ltd, Bodmin

British Library Cataloguing in Publication Data
A catalogue record for this book is available from the British Library

Library of Congress Cataloging in Publication Data
A catalog record for this book has been requested

ISBN 0–415–34717–3

CONTENTS

INTRODUCTION

If you are an English-speaking learner preparing GCSE, Scottish Standard Grade (credit level) or similar examination, or simply learning the language for everyday use, this grammar and workbook is for you. You will typically be either following a course at school, college or evening class, or teaching yourself from a published course. This book is not itself a course, but a self-help reference/revision grammar, with exercises designed to reinforce your grasp of the points dealt with, unit by unit. You will find it a help to have access to a good Italian–English dictionary when working through the book.

Since this is not a self-contained course, the grammar points are usually given on their own, out of context. Of course, this is artificial, because, in everyday life, when we say or write something it is always in a situation or context. To compensate for this artificiality, the grammar points are illustrated with abundant examples, which are often reused, with variations, under different headings. This is partly to strengthen your grasp of grammar and vocabulary, but mostly to help you learn how to manipulate the Italian language in a wide range of situations. Giving plenty of examples is a more effective way of helping you develop the ability to communicate in Italian than giving you lists of rules with just one or two examples.

At the end of each unit, there are several sets of exercises. If you work through these, you will find that they consolidate your understanding of the various points introduced in the unit, and also that they give you the confidence to have a go at expressing yourself in a range of situations and contexts.

The aim of the examples and exercises is to strengthen awareness of the specific points dealt with in the unit; they are not intended to cover all the possible uses of a given word or grammatical structure.

At the end of the book, there is a key to all the exercises, and a glossary of grammatical terms, with examples.

SIGNS AND ABBREVIATIONS

f   feminine
fp   feminine plural
fs   feminine singular
lit.   literally
m   masculine
mp   masculine plural
ms   masculine singular
pl.   plural
sing.   singular

Square brackets indicate an explanatory comment attached to an example, e.g.

C'è Luisa al telefono. [i.e. she has just rung]	That's Luisa on the phone.
Quanto zucchero [ms] **vuoi?**	How much sugar do you want?
'Dov'è Anna?' 'No lo so.'	'Where's Anna?' 'I don't know.' [lit. I don't know it]

Round brackets in an example show that the material in brackets is optional, e.g.

'Hai i libri?' 'Sì, (ce) li ho.'	'Have you got the books?' 'Yes, I've got them.'
Ne ho mangiati due.	I ate two (of them).
A chi scrivete?	Who(m) are you writing to?

Round brackets round an entire sentence show that, while possible, this is a formal form that is not often used, e.g.

((Loro) Partono, Signori Bianco?)	Are you leaving(, Mr and Mrs Bianco)?

A slash shows alternative ways of saying something, e.g.

Gli dico/Dico loro la verità. I tell them the truth. (Here, **gli dico** and **dico loro** are alternative ways of saying 'I tell them'.)
Non mi sembra giusto. It doesn't seem fair to me/I don't think it's fair. (Here, the English sentences are alternatives to one another.)

UNIT ONE
Nouns: gender and number

Gender: masculine and feminine

1 All Italian nouns are either masculine or feminine. The best way to remember the gender of a noun is to learn it along with its definite article (i.e. the word meaning 'the'). In this unit, nouns will therefore be given along with their definite articles, but there will be no discussion of the articles as such. Definite and indefinite articles are the subject of Unit 2.

Most nouns in the singular end in **-o**, **-a**, or **-e**.

2 Italian nouns ending in **-o** are usually masculine:

l'uomo [m]	man
il fratello [m]	brother
il pomeriggio [m]	afternoon
il treno [m]	train

3 Italian nouns ending in **-a** are usually feminine:

la donna [f]	woman
la sorella [f]	sister
la sera [f]	evening
la bicicletta [f]	bicycle

4 Italian nouns ending in **-e** can be either masculine or feminine. Unless a noun ending in **-e** denotes a person whose gender is defined (e.g. 'husband', 'wife'), there are virtually no rules to determine its gender, which must therefore be learned by heart or checked in a dictionary:

Masculine		Feminine	
il padre	father	**la madre**	mother
il ristorante	restaurant	**la notte**	night
il sale	salt	**la luce**	light
il cognome	surname	**la chiave**	key

To help you to determine the gender of some nouns ending in **-e**, here is a rule: nouns ending in **-sione** or **-zione** are feminine:

la televisione [f]	television
la pensione [f]	pension
la produzione [f]	production
la stazione [f]	station

Sometimes, the gender of a noun ending in **-e** can be determined by the gender of the person it refers to: masculine when it refers to a male, feminine when it refers to a female:

il/la cantante [m/f]	(male/female) singer
il/la cliente [m/f]	(male/female) customer
il/la parente [m/f]	(male/female) relative
l'inglese [m/f]	Englishman/Englishwoman

5 Some nouns ending in **-a** and referring to persons are masculine when they refer to a male and feminine when they refer to a female:*

il/la collega [m/f]	(male/female) colleague
l'atleta [m/f]	(male/female) athlete
il/la batterista [m/f]	(male/female) drummer
il/la pianista [m/f]	(male/female) pianist

* There are some exceptions: e.g. **la persona** (person) and **la guida** (tourist guide) are always feminine, even when they refer to a male, while the feminine of **il poeta** (poet) is **la poetessa**.

6 There are some nouns ending in **-a** which are masculine and some nouns ending in **-o** which are feminine:

Masculine		Feminine	
il cinema	cinema	**l'auto**	car
il papà	dad	**la foto**	photo
il problema	problem	**la mano**	hand

Some nouns of this type are abbreviations, and have kept the gender of the full word: **cinema** stands for **cinematografo** [m], **auto** for **automobile** [f], **foto** for **fotografia** [f], etc. Such cases apart, there is no rule for determining gender, which has to be learned by heart or checked in a dictionary.

7 Some nouns end in **-i**. The vast majority are feminine, but there are some exceptions:

l'analisi [f]	analysis
l'ipotesi [f]	hypothesis
la crisi [f]	crisis

Two exceptions are **l'alibi** (alibi) and **lo sci** (ski), which are masculine.

8 Foreign nouns, unless they refer to a female, are generally masculine:

il bar [m]	bar
il camion [m]	lorry
il rock [m]	rock (music)
l'hostess [f]	stewardess

9 Occasionally, the gender of a foreign noun is the same as it is for the corresponding Italian word:

la new wave is feminine, because **onda** (wave) is feminine.
la mail (e-mail message) is feminine, because **posta** (mail) is feminine.

10 The following rules can help in determining the gender of nouns:

- All months of the year and days of the week are masculine, apart from **domenica** (Sunday), which is feminine.
- All names of towns and cities are feminine, apart from **Il Cairo** [m].
- All names of languages are masculine.
- Names of countries are normally feminine when they end in **-a** and masculine when they end in any other letter:

la Francia [f]	France
la Spagna [f]	Spain
il Belgio [m]	Belgium
il Paraguay [m]	Paraguay

Number: singular and plural

11 Masculine nouns ending in **-o**, and all nouns ending in **-e**, end in **-i** in the plural:

Singular		*Plural*	
il treno [m]	train	**i treni**	trains
il nome [m]	name/noun	**i nomi**	names/nouns
la notte [f]	night	**le notti**	nights
la stazione [f]	station	**le stazioni**	stations
la pensione [f]	pension	**le pensioni**	pensions
il/la parente [m/f]	relative	**i/le parenti**	relatives
la moglie [f]	wife	**le mogli***	wives

* Nouns ending in **-ie** have only one **-i** in the plural.

12 Nouns ending in **-io** have only one **i** in the plural. But if the **-i** is stressed (**-*io***), the plural has two (**-*ii***):

Singular		*Plural*	
il bacio [m]	kiss	**i baci**	kisses
il desiderio [m]	wish	**i desideri**	wishes
l'inizio [m]	beginning	**gli inizi**	beginnings
lo z*io* [m]	uncle	**gli z*ii***	uncles
il mormor*io* [m]	murmur	**i mormor*ii***	murmurs

13 Feminine nouns ending in **-a** take **-e** in the plural:

Singular		*Plural*	
la sorella [f]	sister	**le sorelle**	sisters
la lettera [f]	letter	**le lettere**	letters
la sera [f]	evening	**le sere**	evenings

14 Masculine nouns ending in **-a** take **-i** in the plural:

Singular		*Plural*	
il problema [m]	problem	**i problemi**	problems
il sistema [m]	system	**i sistemi**	systems

15 When a noun ending in **-a** denotes a person, its plural ending depends on whether it is masculine or feminine. If it refers to a male, the plural ends in **-i**; if it refers to a female, the plural ends in **-e**:

Singular	Plural
il pianista [m] (male) pianist	**i pianisti** [m] (male) pianists
la pianista [f] (female) pianist	**le pianiste** [f] (female) pianists
il collega [m] (male) colleague	**i colleghi*** [m] (male) colleagues
la collega [f] (female) colleague	**le colleghe*** [f] (female) colleagues

* For an explanation of the **-h-** in these endings, see paragraph 20 below.

16 Nouns ending in **-i** do not change in the plural:

Singular		Plural	
l'analisi [f]	analysis	**le analisi**	analyses
la crisi [f]	crisis	**le crisi**	crises

17 Foreign nouns, and nouns stressed on the last vowel, do not change in the plural:

Singular		Plural	
il bar [m]	bar	**i bar**	bars
lo sport [m]	sport	**gli sport**	sports
la città [f]	city	**le città**	cities
la virtù [f]	virtue	**le virtù**	virtues

18 A number of nouns are irregular in the plural. E.g. **la mano** [f] (hand) becomes **le mani** in the plural, **l'uomo** [m] (man) becomes **gli uomini** in the plural. Here are some nouns which do not change in the plural, because they are abbreviations (cf. above, paragraph 6):

Singular		Plural	
l'auto [f]	car	**le auto**	cars
la radio [f]	radio	**le radio**	radios
la moto [f]	motorbike	**le moto**	motorbikes
la foto [f]	photo	**le foto**	photos
il cinema [m]	cinema	**i cinema**	cinemas

Some nouns are masculine in the singular but feminine in the plural. Here are a few:

Singular		Plural	
il dito [m]	finger	**le dita** [f]	fingers
il centinaio [m]	(about) a hundred	**le centinaia** [f]	hundreds
il migliaio [m]	(about) a thousand	**le migliaia** [f]	thousands
il miglio [m]	mile	**le miglia** [f]	miles
il paio [m]	pair	**le paia** [f]	pairs
l'uovo [m]	egg	**le uova** [f]	eggs

19 Note that, in Italian, the masculine form of a noun is also used when the gender is not important. A noun in the plural may therefore designate any one of three different sets of people:

gli amici	*either* a specific set of male friends [as in 'Your friends (Luigi and Giovanni) have arrived.']
	or a specific mixed set of male and female friends [as in 'Your friends (Luigi and Anna) have arrived.']
	or friends in general [whether male and female does not matter, as in 'Everybody needs friends.']
gli insegnanti	*either* a specific set of male teachers
	or a specific mixed set of male and female teachers
	or teachers in general [regardless of gender]
i colleghi	*either* a specific set of male colleagues
	or a specific mixed set of male and female colleagues
	or colleagues in general [regardless of gender]

Spelling

Care is needed in spelling some plurals.

20 Nouns ending in **-ca** or **-ga** always add **h** (**-che** or **-ghe**), in order to keep the hard sound of **c** and **g** in the plural. We saw the example of **il/la collega** in paragraph 15. Here are some more:

Singular		*Plural*	
l'amica [f]	(female) friend	**le amiche**	(female) friends
la tasca [f]	pocket	**le tasche**	pockets
la riga [f]	line, ruler	**le righe**	lines, rulers

21 Nouns ending in **-co** and **-go** normally add **h** (**-chi** or **-ghi**) and keep the hard sound, but some nouns change the sound of **c** and **g** in the plural (**-ci** or **-gi**). It is always best to check in a dictionary:

Singular		*Plural*	
il bosco [m]	wood	**i boschi**	woods
il gioco [m]	game	**i giochi**	games
il parco [m]	park	**i parchi**	parks
il lago [m]	lake	**i laghi**	lakes
l'amico [m]	(male) friend	**gli amici**	(male) friends
il medico [m]	doctor	**i medici**	doctors
il biologo [m]	biologist	**i biologi**	biologists

22 Nouns ending in **-cia** or **-gia** keep the **i** in the plural (**-cie** or **-gie**) when the **i** is stressed, or when **c** or **g** is preceded by a vowel. But if **-cia** or **-gia** is preceded by a consonant the **i** is lost in the plural:

Singular		*Plural*	
la farmac*i*a [f]	pharmacy	**le farmac*i*e**	pharmacies
la bug*i*a [f]	lie	**le bug*i*e**	lies
la camicia [f]	shirt/blouse	**le camicie**	shirts/blouses
la ciliegia [f]	cherry	**le ciliegie**	cherries
l'arancia [f]	orange	**le arance**	oranges
la doccia [f]	shower	**le docce**	showers
la spiaggia [f]	beach	**le spiagge**	beaches

Exercise 1

With the help of a dictionary where necessary, decide what gender the nouns are, and write m, f or m/f after each one.

Examples: la notte f; il/la pianista m/f; il fratello m

1	il giorno _____	11	l'uovo _____
2	la sera _____	12	la camicia _____
3	l'uomo _____	13	l'atleta _____
4	l'infermiera _____	14	l'animale _____
5	la stanza _____	15	la strada _____
6	l'orecchio _____	16	l'acqua _____
7	il caffè _____	17	l'abitante _____
8	lo zucchero _____	18	l'occhio _____
9	il fiume _____	19	il sole _____
10	l'olandese _____	20	la canzone _____

Exercise 2

With the help of a dictionary where necessary, fill in the plurals of the nouns.

Examples: la notte: le notti; il nome: i nomi; il treno: i treni;
            la sera: le sere

1 il ragazzo	i _____	11 la banca	le _____
2 la marca	le _____	12 il pianista	i _____
3 la chiave	le _____	13 la cliente	le _____
4 l'abitante	gli _____	14 l'indirizzo	gli _____
5 lo zio	gli _____	15 l'occhio	gli _____
6 il fiume	i _____	16 il ristorante	i _____
7 la stazione	le _____	17 la televisione	le _____
8 la ragazza	le _____	18 il calendario	i _____
9 l'energia	le _____	19 il francese	i _____
10 il pomeriggio	i _____	20 il lago	i _____

Exercise 3

With the help of a dictionary where necessary, fill in the singulars of the nouns.

Examples: la <u>casa</u>: le case; il <u>libro</u>: i libri; il <u>mese</u>: i mesi;
la <u>moglie</u>: le mogli

1 il _____	i nomi	11 la _____	le ciliegie
2 la _____	le vie	12 il _____	i caffè
3 il _____	i figli	13 il _____	i medici
4 la _____	le mani	14 l'_____	gli attivisti
5 l'_____	le opinioni	15 il _____	le ginocchia
6 il _____	i clienti	16 la _____	le bugie
7 l'_____	gli occhi	17 il _____	i tedeschi
8 la _____	le persone	18 il _____	i test
9 la _____	le marche	19 l'_____	gli uomini
10 il _____	i problemi	20 l'_____	le amiche

UNIT TWO
Definite and indefinite articles

Definite article

1 In Italian the definite article (English 'the') has different forms, depending on the gender (masculine/feminine) and number (singular/plural) of the following word, and on the letter (or sound) with which the following word begins. Here are the forms:

	Singular	*Plural*	
Feminine	la	le	
	l'	le	
Masculine	il	i	} the
	lo	gli	
	l'	gli	

2 The feminine forms are used before feminine words, **la** and **l'** for the singular, and **le** for the plural:

la is used before words beginning with a consonant;
l' is used before words beginning with a vowel (**a, e, i, o, u**) or **h**;
le is used as the plural for both **la** and **l'**:

Singular	*Plural*	
la ragazza	**le ragazze**	the girl(s)
la casa	**le case**	the house(s)
la stanza	**le stanze**	the room(s)
l'auto	**le auto**	the car(s)
l'esperienza	**le esperienze**	the experience(s)
l'hostess	**le hostess**	the stewardess(es)

3 There are three different forms for the masculine singular: **il**, **lo** and **l'**; and two for the plural: **i** and **gli**. All these forms are used before masculine words:

l' is used before words beginning with a vowel or **h**;
lo is used before words starting with **z**, **gn**, **ps**, **s** + consonant;
il is used in all other cases;
i is used as the plural of **il**;
gli is used as the plural of both **l'** and **lo**:

Singular	*Plural*	
l'articolo	**gli articoli**	the article(s)
l'uomo	**gli uomini**	the man/men
l'hotel	**gli hotel**	the hotel(s)
lo zio	**gli zii**	the uncle(s)
lo gnomo	**gli gnomi**	the gnome(s)
lo psicologo	**gli psicologi**	the psychologist(s)
lo chef*	**gli chef***	the chef(s)
lo spettacolo	**gli spettacoli**	the show(s)
lo sciopero	**gli scioperi**	the strike(s)
il bar	**i bar**	the bar(s)
il ristorante	**i ristoranti**	the restaurant(s)
il senso	**i sensi**	the sense(s)

* The use of **lo/gli** is due to the initial sound of **chef**, pronounced in Italian as in English (i.e. 'sh').

Lo is also used before masculine words starting with **i** + vowel, **x**, **y**:

Singular	*Plural*	
lo ione	**gli ioni**	the ion(s)
lo yuppie	**gli yuppie**	the yuppie(s)
lo xenofobo	**gli xenofobi**	the xenophobe(s)
lo juventino*	**gli juventini***	the Juventus fan(s)

* The use of **lo/gli** is due to the initial sound of **juventino**, pronounced as **i** + vowel (i.e. like the 'y' in English 'youth').

4 Care is needed in using the article with nouns ending in **-e** or **-a** which can refer both to male or female persons (see Unit 1, paragraphs 4 and 5):

Singular		*Plural*	
il cantante [m]	the (male) singer	**i cantanti** [m]	the singers [male, *or* male and female mixed]
la cantante [f]	the (female) singer	**le cantanti** [f]	the (female) singers

Singular		Plural	
l'insegnante [m]	the (male) teacher	**gli insegnanti** [m]	the teachers [male, *or* male and female mixed]
l'insegnante [f]	the (female) teacher	**le insegnanti** [f]	the (female) teachers
il collega [m]	the (male) colleague	**i colleghi** [m]	the colleagues [male, *or* male and female mixed]
la collega [f]	the (female) colleague	**le colleghe** [f]	the (female) colleagues
l'atleta [m]	the (male) athlete	**gli atleti** [m]	the athletes [male, *or* male and female mixed]
l'atleta [f]	the (female) athlete	**le atlete** [f]	the (female) athletes

Remember that, as we saw in Unit 1, paragraph 19, the masculine plural form can also denote a class of people in general, as well as a group of males or a mixed group of males and females: e.g. **i cantanti** [m] can denote *either* a group of male singers, *or* a mixed group of male and female singers, *or* singers in general.

Indefinite article

5 Like the definite article, the indefinite article (English 'a/an') has different forms, depending on the gender of the word it refers to and the letter (or sound) with which the following word begins. There is no plural for the indefinite article. Here are the forms:

Feminine	**un'**	⎫
	una	⎬ a/an
Masculine	**un**	⎪
	uno	⎭

6 The feminine forms **un'** and **una** are used before feminine words:

un' is used before words beginning with a vowel or **h**;
una is used before words beginning with a consonant:

un'auto	a car
un'esperienza	an experience
un'hostess	a stewardess

una ragazza	a girl
una casa	a house
una stanza	a room

7 The masculine forms **uno** and **un** are used before masculine words:

uno is used before words starting with **z, gn, ps, s** + consonant;
un is used before all other words:

uno zio	an uncle
uno gnomo	a gnome
uno psicologo	a psychologist
uno chef	a chef
uno spettacolo	a show
un articolo	an article
un uomo	a man
un hobby	a hobby
un bar	a bar
un ristorante	a restaurant
un senso	a sense

Uno (like **lo**) is also used before masculine words starting with **i** + vowel, **x, y**:

uno ione	an ion
uno yuppie	a yuppie
uno xenofobo	a xenophobe
uno juventino	a Juventus fan

8 As with the definite article, care is needed in choosing the right article to use with nouns ending in **-e** or **-a** which can refer to either male or female persons:

un cantante [m]	a singer (male)
una cantante [f]	a singer (female)
un insegnante [m]*	a teacher (male)
un'insegnante [f]*	a teacher (female)
un collega [m]	a colleague (male)
una collega [f]	a colleague (female)
un atleta [m]*	an athlete (male)
un'atleta [f]*	an athlete (female)

* In the case of nouns starting with a vowel, the only difference between the articles is the apostrophe.

9 It may be useful to compare the use of the definite and indefinite article in table form:

Masculine
un is used when **il** and **l'** are used
uno is used when **lo** is used

Feminine
un' is used when **l'** is used
una is used when **la** is used

Use of the articles

10 The use of the articles is often the same in Italian as in English, but there are cases (mostly concerning the definite article) where the two languages differ. Here are the most common instances:

- In Italian, the definite article is used before a noun used in a general sense:

Amo la musica rock/le vacanze.	I love rock music/holidays.
La musica rock è popolare.	Rock music is popular.
Le vacanze sono sempre troppo corte.	Holidays are always too short.
Il tempo vola.	Time flies.
Le auto inquinano l'ambiente.	Cars pollute the environment.
La disoccupazione è diffusa.	Unemployment is widespread.

- Italian uses the definite article before a title followed by a surname, except when addressing the person directly:

La Signora Urbani è gentile.	Mrs/Ms Urbani is kind.
La Dottoressa Vanni non c'è.	Doctor Vanni isn't here.
Il Dottor* Marchi è occupato.	Doctor Marchi is busy.
Buongiorno, Signor* Carli!	Good morning, Mr Carli!
Buongiorno, Dottore.	Good morning, Doctor.
Scusi, Signore.	Excuse me(, Sir).

* Note that some masculine titles, notably **Signore**, **Professore** and **Dottore**, drop the final vowel when used before the name of the person, becoming **Signor**, **Professor**, **Dottor**, etc.

- The Italian definite article is always used with years, e.g. **il 1990, il 2000**.
- The definite article is normally used in Italian with names of countries and regions, e.g. **l'Inghilterra** (England), **la Toscana** (Tuscany), **il Portogallo** (Portugal), **l'Europa** (Europe). But the rule may be different when using a preposition, e.g. **in Italia** (in Italy) (see Unit 8, paragraph 14).

11 In some cases a definite article is used in Italian where an indefinite article (or a possessive adjective – see Unit 3) is used in English. Here are some instances:

Antonio ha *il* naso lungo.	Antonio has a long nose.
Hai *la* patente?	Have you got a driving licence?
Avete *l'*ombrello?	Have you got an umbrella?
Ho *il* raffreddore.	I have got a cold.
Dove passi *le* vacanze di solito?	Where do you normally spend your holidays?
Di pomeriggio faccio *il* compito.	In the afternoon I do my homework.
Hai *il* biglietto?	Have you got a/your ticket?

There are also cases when there is no article in Italian but the definite or indefinite article is used in English:

Andiamo in montagna.	We're going to the mountains.
Stasera andiamo a teatro.	We're going to the theatre this evening.
Accompagno Anna in aeroporto.	I'm taking Anna to the airport.
Andiamo in macchina.	We're going in the/a car.
Carlo è medico.	Carlo is a doctor.
Sono studente.	I'm a student.
Non ha marito.	She hasn't got a husband.

Definite and indefinite article before an adjective

12 As we shall see (Unit 3), a noun can sometimes be preceded by an adjective, so that the adjective comes between the article and the noun (e.g. **una *bella* donna**, a beautiful woman). In such cases, the form of the article depends on the spelling of the *adjective*, not the noun:

la casa	the house	**l'ultima casa**	the last house
una casa	a house	**un'ottima casa**	an excellent house
l'auto	the car	**la prima auto**	the first car
un'auto	a car	**una bella auto**	a beautiful car

Exercise 1

Insert the definite article before the nouns.

Examples: l'acqua; la stanza; le esperienze; il ristorante; lo zio;
gli uomini

1 ____ figlia		11 ____ notti
2 ____ zia		12 ____ sport
3 ____ problema		13 ____ uovo
4 ____ mano		14 ____ xenofobia
5 ____ auto		15 ____ tivù
6 ____ fratello		16 ____ amici
7 ____ libri		17 ____ pianiste
8 ____ entrata		18 ____ dita
9 ____ studio		19 ____ crisi
10 ____ zii		20 ____ inglese

Exercise 2

Insert the indefinite article before the nouns.

Examples: un'auto; una ragazza; un articolo; uno spettacolo;
un insegnante [m]; un'atleta [f]

1 ____ sorella		11 ____ arancia
2 ____ ciliegia		12 ____ psichiatra [m]
3 ____ amico		13 ____ sigaretta
4 ____ zio		14 ____ insegnante [f]
5 ____ zia		15 ____ gnu
6 ____ aereo		16 ____ artista [m]
7 ____ amica		17 ____ sbaglio
8 ____ cantante [f]		18 ____ figlio
9 ____ migliaio		19 ____ yogurt
10 ____ specchio		20 ____ analisi

Exercise 3

Insert the correct article in the blank spaces.

Example: Maria ha <u>una</u> casa. (Maria has a house.)

1 ____ zio di Maria arriva domani. (Maria's uncle arrives tomorrow.)
2 Paolo scrive ____ lettera. (Paolo is writing a letter.)
3 Hai ____ mani pulite? (Have you got clean hands?)
4 È ____ amica di Patrizia. (She's a friend of Patrizia's.)
5 Laura non ha ____ patente. (Laura hasn't got a driving licence.)
6 C'è ____ Signor Totti? (Is Mr Totti here?)
7 È ____ insegnante molto capace. (She's a very capable teacher.)
8 ____ inquinamento è ____ problema preoccupante. (Pollution is a
   worrying problem.)
9 ____ nuovo stadio è più grande. (The new stadium is bigger.)
10 Ho ____ stesso CD. (I've got the same CD.)

UNIT THREE
Adjectives; possessive and demonstrative pronouns

1 Adjectives in Italian must agree in gender and number with the noun they refer to: if the noun is masculine singular the adjective must be masculine singular, if the noun is feminine singular the adjective must be feminine singular, etc. Adjectives therefore change their forms accordingly. But remember that when an adjective is listed in a dictionary or a grammar, it is given in its masculine singular form. In the masculine singular, most Italian adjectives end in **-o** or in **-e**:

italiano	Italian
nuovo	new
francese	French
grande	big

2 Adjectives ending in **-o** have four different forms: **-o** for the masculine singular (**italiano**), **-a** for feminine singular (**italiana**), **-i** for the masculine plural (**italiani**) and **-e** for the feminine plural (**italiane**):

l'arbitro [ms] **italiano**	the Italian referee
gli arbitri [mp] **italiani**	the Italian referees
la cameriera [fs] **italiana**	the Italian waitress
le cameriere [fp] **italiane**	the Italian waitresses
lo stadio [ms] **nuovo**	the new stadium
gli stadi [mp] **nuovi**	the new stadia/stadiums
la casa [fs] **nuova**	the new house
le case [fp] **nuove**	the new houses

3 Adjectives ending in **-e** have only two forms: **-e** for the masculine and feminine singular (**francese**) and **-i** for the masculine and feminine plural (**francesi**). With adjectives ending in **-e** there is thus no difference between the masculine and the feminine form:

l'arbitro [ms] **francese**	the French referee
gli arbitri [mp] **francesi**	the French referees
la cameriera [fs] **francese**	the French waitress
le cameriere [fp] **francesi**	the French waitresses
lo stadio [ms] **grande**	the big stadium
gli stadi [mp] **grandi**	the big stadia/stadiums
la casa [fs] **grande**	the big house
le case [fp] **grandi**	the big houses

4 Some adjectives end in **-a**, like the following:

ottimista	optimistic
pacifista	pacifist
belga	Belgian
entusiasta	enthusiastic
idiota	idiotic

These adjectives have three forms: **-a** for the masculine and feminine singular (**ottimista**), **-i** for the masculine plural (**ottimisti**) and **-e** for the feminine plural (**ottimiste**). There is thus only one form for the masculine and feminine singular:

il corteo [ms] **pacifista**	the pacifist rally
l'idea [fs] **pacifista**	the pacifist idea
i cortei [mp] **pacifisti**	the pacifist rallies
le idee [fp] **pacifiste**	the pacifist ideas
il ragazzo [ms] **belga**	the Belgian boy
la ragazza [fs] **belga**	the Belgian girl
i ragazzi [mp] **belgi**	the Belgian boys
le ragazze [fp] **belghe***	the Belgian girls

* For an explanation of the **-h-** in **belghe**, see paragraph 6 below.

5 There are also some invariable adjectives, e.g. **blu** (dark blue), **rosa** (pink), **dispari** (odd), **pari** (even), which do not change.

il vestito rosa	the pink garment/dress/suit
la penna blu	the blue pen
i numeri dispari	the odd numbers
le pagine pari	the even pages

6 Care is needed in spelling the plural of adjectives ending in **-co** and **-go**. There is no fixed rule for the masculine forms, which may keep the hard

sound of **c** and **g** and add **h** (**-chi, -ghi**), or change the sound of **c** and **g** in the plural (**-ci, -gi**). The feminine plural forms always add **h** (**-che, -ghe**) in order to keep the hard sound of **c** and **g**. If in doubt, check in a dictionary; the best way to remember these sorts of plural is through practice:

Masculine singular	Masculine plural	Feminine singular	Feminine plural	
greco	greci	greca	greche	Greek
pratico	pratici	pratica	pratiche	practical
pubblico	pubblici	pubblica	pubbliche	public
ricco	ricchi	ricca	ricche	rich
fresco	freschi	fresca	fresche	fresh
largo	larghi	larga	larghe	wide

The adjective **belga**, as we have seen, keeps the hard sound of **g** in the feminine plural by adding **h** (**belghe**); but it changes the sound in the masculine plural (**belgi**).

7 As can be seen in the examples, the adjective normally comes after the noun it refers to and (unless it is invariable) it must agree in gender and number with the noun. It must also agree in gender and number with the noun even where it is separated from it by another word, such as a verb:

Lorenzo è italiano.	Lorenzo is Italian.
Lorenzo e Vittorio sono italiani.	Lorenzo and Vittorio are Italian.
Anna è italiana.	Anna is Italian.
Anna e Claudia sono italiane.	Anna and Claudia are Italian.

When the adjective refers to two or more nouns which are different in gender, it is masculine plural:

Lorenzo, Anna e Claudia sono italiani.	Lorenzo, Anna and Claudia are Italian.
Sabine e Kurt sono tedeschi.	Sabine and Kurt are German.
Il computer e la stampante sono nuovi.	The computer and the printer are new.
Il bagno e la cucina sono piccoli.	The bathroom and the kitchen are small.
I pantaloni e la camicia sono nuovi.	The trousers and the shirt are new.

8 In some cases the adjective can also precede the noun it refers to. When the adjective comes before the noun, the meaning of the noun becomes different, as in these examples:

un vecchio amico	an old [i.e. long-standing] friend
un amico vecchio	an old/elderly friend [i.e. a friend who is old]
la povera donna	the poor [i.e. unfortunate] woman
la donna povera	the poor woman [i.e. she has no money]

9 The demonstrative adjectives **questo** (this) and **quello** (that), like their English counterparts, always precede the noun they refer to:

questo ragazzo	this boy
questa ragazza	this girl
questi ragazzi	these boys
queste ragazze	these girls
quel* ragazzo	that boy
quella* ragazza	that girl
quei* ragazzi	those boys
quelle* ragazze	those girls

* For an explanation of the forms of **quello**, see paragraph 10.

10 The forms of the adjectives **quello** and **bello** (beautiful/handsome/nice/-fine) change in the same way as the definite article. Here are the forms, followed in brackets by the corresponding forms of the definite article:

	Singular		*Plural*	
Masculine	**quel/bel**	**(il)**	**quei/bei**	**(i)**
	quello/bello	**(lo)**	**quegli/begli**	**(gli)**
	quell'/bell'	**(l')**	**quegli/begli**	**(gli)**
Feminine	**quella/bella**	**(la)**	**quelle/belle**	**(le)**
	quell'/bell'*	**(l')**	**quelle/belle**	**(le)**

* The feminine singular form **bell'** is rarely used, and **bella** is preferred, even before a vowel.

quel film	that film	**bei film**	beautiful films
bello spettacolo	lovely show	**quegli spettacoli**	those shows
quell'esempio	that example	**begli esempi**	fine examples
quella canzone	that song	**belle canzoni**	beautiful songs
bella esperienza	beautiful experience	**quelle esperienze**	those experiences
quel bel film	that beautiful film	**quei bei film**	those beautiful films

Note that when **bello** comes *after* the noun, the full form is used: **lo spettacolo è bello, un'esperienza bella e interessante**, etc.

11 The forms of the adjective **buono** (good), when used before a singular noun, change in the same way as the indefinite article:

Masculine	**buon**	(**un**)
	buono	(**uno**)
Feminine	**buon'/buona***	(**un'**)
	buona	(**una**)

* Nowadays the form **buona** is preferred to **buon'**.

buon libro	good book	**buona idea**	good idea
buon amico	good friend	**buona esperienza**	good experience
buon caffè	good coffee	**buona memoria**	good memory
buono studente	good student		

Note that when **buono** comes *after* the noun, the full form is used: **questo libro è buono, il caffè è buono**, etc.

12 The adjective **grande** (big/great), when used before the noun, may change to the invariable form **gran** or, in some expressions, to **grand'**; nowadays, the full form, **grande**, is preferred in most cases:

grande musicista	**gran musicista**	great musician
grande film	**gran film**	great film
grande casa	**gran casa**	big house
	Gran Bretagna	Great Britain
grande amico	[sometimes] **grand'amico/gran amico**	great friend
grande idea	[sometimes] **grand'idea/gran idea**	great idea
[sometimes] **grande uomo**	**grand'uomo**	great man

Note that before *plural* nouns, **grande** is regular: **grandi musicisti, grandi case,** etc.

Note also that when **grande** comes *after* the noun, the full form is always used: **quel film è grande, la casa è grande**, etc.

13 The adjective **santo** (saint) is another that has different forms when used before a noun:

santo is only used before masculine names starting with **s** + consonant;
san is used before masculine names starting with a consonant (other than **s** + consonant);
sant' is used before masculine or feminine names starting with a vowel;
santa is used before feminine names starting with a consonant:

Santo Stefano	Saint Stephen	**Sant'Antonio**	Saint Anthony
San Francesco	Saint Francis	**Sant'Anna**	Saint Anne
San Pietro	Saint Peter	**Santa Caterina**	Saint Catherine

Note that when **santo** means 'holy' or 'blessed', it is regular: **il santo padre** (the Holy Father), **una santa donna** (a holy woman).

Possessive adjectives and pronouns

14 The forms of the possessive adjectives ('my', 'your', etc.) are as follows:

Masculine singular	Feminine singular	Masculine plural	Feminine plural	
mio	**mia**	**miei***	**mie**	my
tuo	**tua**	**tuoi***	**tue**	your
suo	**sua**	**suoi***	**sue**	his/her/its
nostro	**nostra**	**nostri**	**nostre**	our
vostro	**vostra**	**vostri**	**vostre**	your
loro**	**loro****	**loro****	**loro****	their

* Note that the masculine plural forms **miei**, **tuoi** and **suoi** are irregular.
** Note that **loro** is invariable and does not change.

Possessive adjectives are always used before the noun they refer to. Unlike in English, they are always preceded by the article, and they must agree with the owned object, not with the owner:

Luisa e *i* su*oi* fratelli [mp]	Luisa and her brothers
Carlo e *le* su*e* sorelle [fp]	Carlo and his sisters
Livia e *il* su*o* amico [ms]	Livia and her (male) friend
Ettore e *la* su*a* amica [fs]	Ettore and his (female) friend
***la* mi*a* lettera** [fs]	my letter
***i* tu*oi* libri** [mp]	your books
***la* nostr*a* scuola** [fs]	our school
***le* vostr*e* idee** [fp]	your ideas
***la* loro stanza** [fs]	their room
***i* loro genitori** [mp]	their parents

15 When **mio**, **tuo**, **suo**, **nostro** and **vostro** (*not* **loro**) are used with a noun denoting family relationship (e.g. **fratello** (brother), **sorella** (sister), **padre** (father), **madre** (mother)) in the singular they are *not* preceded by the definite article:

mio padre	my father
tua madre	your mother
tuo fratello	your brother
sua zia	his/her aunt
i tuoi fratelli [pl.]	your brothers
le sue zie [pl.]	his/her aunts
il loro padre	their father

16 The forms of the possessive pronouns ('mine', 'yours', etc.) are the same as those of the possessive adjectives, and are always preceded by the definite article:

Masculine singular	Feminine singular	Masculine plural	Feminine plural	
il mio	**la mia**	**i miei**	**le mie**	mine
il tuo	**la tua**	**i tuoi**	**le tue**	yours
il suo	**la sua**	**i suoi**	**le sue**	his/hers/its
il nostro	**la nostra**	**i nostri**	**le nostre**	ours
il vostro	**la vostra**	**i vostri**	**le vostre**	yours
il loro	**la loro**	**i loro**	**le loro**	theirs

La tua casa è grande, ma *la loro* è piccola.	Your house is big, but theirs is small.
I tuoi CD sono qui, *i nostri* sono lì.	Your CDs are here, ours are there.

17 As we shall see (Unit 4, paragraph 5), in Italian there is a form used to address people formally. In the formal way of addressing people, the possessive adjectives and pronouns used are **Suo** for the singular, and **Vostro** (or **Loro** if a higher degree of formality is required) for the plural:

Adjectives

La *Sua* auto è pronta, Signora Ferrero.	Your car's ready, Mrs Ferrero.
Ecco *i Suoi* libri, Signore.	Here are your books(, Sir).
Signori Bianco, *la Vostra* stanza è pronta.	(Mr and Mrs Bianco,) your room is ready.
(Signori Bianco, *la Loro* stanza è pronta.)	

Pronouns

La loro auto è in strada, ma *la Sua* è in garage, Signora.	Their car's in the street, but yours is in the garage(, Madam).
Professore, questi libri sono *i Suoi*.	These books are yours(, Professor/Sir).

Questa stanza è *la Vostra*, Signori Bianco.	This room is yours(, Mr and Mrs Bianco).
(Questa stanza è *la Loro*, Signori Bianco.)	(This room is yours, Mr and Mrs Bianco.)

Demonstrative pronouns

18 **Questo** and **quello** are also used as demonstrative pronouns (this (one), that (one), these (ones), those (ones)). But note that when **quello** is used as a demonstrative pronoun, its endings are not modelled on the definite article (cf. paragraph 10), but are the same as those of **questo** (i.e. **quell*o*** [ms], **quell*a*** [fs], **quell*i*** [mp], **quell*e*** [fp]):

Questa è Anna.	This is Anna.
Questa è la tua stanza e quella è la mia.	This is my room and that one's yours.
Questi sono gli esercizi.	These are the exercises.
Quello è il nuovo computer.	That is the new computer.
Quelle sono le Alpi.	Those are the Alps.
Questi biscotti sono buoni, ma preferisco quelli.	These biscuits are nice, but I prefer those.

Exercise 1

Complete the phrases by choosing the form of the adjective that agrees with the noun.

Examples: le ragazze (italiano) <u>italiane</u>; (quello) acqua (caldo) <u>quell'</u>, <u>calda</u>.

1   un libro (interessante) _____
2   la gonna (bianco) _____
3   i vestiti (bianco) _____
4   le camicie (rosso) _____
5   gli insegnanti (egoista) _____
6   un (bello) albero _____
7   un collega (razzista) _____
8   le situazioni (comico) _____
9   le donne (simpatico) _____
10   i capelli (lungo) _____

11 (quello) ragazzo (simpatico) _____
12 (questo) esercizi (facile) _____
13 (quello) (bello) specchi _____
14 (questo) (bello) donne _____
15 (quello) alberi (morto) _____
16 (questo) amici (inglese)_____
17 (quello) attiviste (spagnolo) _____
18 (quello) (bello) attore _____
19 (quello) uova (fresco) _____
20 (quello) turisti (greco) _____

Exercise 2

Choose the right adjective for each noun or pair of nouns.

> Examples: Queste scarpe sono (rossa/nuove/belli) <u>nuove</u>; Anna e Franco
> sono (francese/italiane/italiani) <u>italiani</u>.

1   La casa è (vecchio/nuovi/grande). _____
2   Ho un vestito (rosa/nuova/lunghe). _____
3   Le professoresse sono (intelligente/francesi/noiosa). _____
4   La crisi è (seriose/violenti/grave). _____
5   I colleghi (italiane/ottimista/pacifisti) arrivano domani. _____
6   Queste macchine sono (veloce/nuovi/tedesche). _____
7   Questo bambino è (capricciose/pigro/beneducata). _____
8   Quei film sono (inglese/divertente/lunghi). _____
9   Le cameriere sono (giovane/greca/belghe). _____
10 Il pianista non è (stanca/belga/vecchi). _____
11 Ho le dita (puliti/sporche/lunghi). _____
12 Quel signore ha un carattere (simpatiche/cortesi/energico). _____
13 Questi blue-jeans sono (resistenti/pratiche/americana). _____
14 Le maglie sono (vecchio/blu/bianchi). _____
15 Le cantanti sono (spagnoli/tedeschi/scozzesi). _____
16 Il treno e l'auto sono (veloci/inquinante/comodo). _____
17 Paola, Claudia e Anna sono (italiani/belli/simpatiche). _____
18 Claudio e Patrizia sono (gentile/italiani/contenta). _____
19 Gianfranco, Piero e Giorgio sono (felice/ottimisti/italiane). _____
20 I signori e le signore sono (soddisfatti/greco/affollate). _____

Exercise 3

Complete the sentences by adding the correct form of the possessive adjective and, where necessary, the article.

Examples: Conosco Luisa e (suo) fratelli: <u>i suoi</u>; (Mio) madre è bella: <u>Mia</u>

1 (Loro) bambini sono cortesi. _____
2 (Suo) occhi sono blu. _____
3 Questa è (mio) bici. _____
4 Quanti anni hanno (tuo) sorelle? _____
5 (Vostro) macchina è nuova? _____
6 (Nostro) lavoro è interessante. _____
7 (Mio) amici sono in vacanza. _____
8 (Loro) casa è grande. _____
9 (Tuo) madre è simpatica. _____
10 Grazie per (Suo) lettera, Signore. _____

Exercise 4

Answer the questions, using possessive pronouns.

Example: 'È la Sua macchina, Signor Rossi?' 'Sì, è <u>la mia.</u>'

1 'È il cellulare di Anna?' 'No, non è _____.'
2 'È la Vostra casa, Signori Zola?' 'Sì, è _____.'
3 'Sono i miei CD?' 'No, non sono _____.'
4 'È il Suo ufficio?' 'No, non è _____.'
5 'Sono i suoi libri?' 'Sì, sono _____.'
6 'Sono le mie lettere?' 'Sì, sono _____.'
7 'È la casa dei tuoi amici?' 'Sì, è _____.'
8 'Sono i nostri vestiti?' 'No, non sono _____.'
9 'Sono le camicie di Paolo?' 'Sì, sono _____.'
10 'Sono i vostri bagagli?' 'Sì, sono _____.'

Exercise 5

Complete the sentences by choosing the right form of the adjectives and pronouns.

    Example: (Questo) non è (tuo) stanza, è (mio): Questa non è la tua stanza, è la mia.

1 (Questo) signori sono (nostro) ospiti (tedesco).
2 (Suo) colleghi sono (ottimista), Signora!
3 (Questo) sono (vostro) stanze.
4 Io ho (mio) documenti, Lei ha (Suo), Signore?
5 (Questo) sono (mio) CD, (quello) sono (tuo).
6 (Nostro) professore è (entusiasta), com'è (vostro)?
7 (Quello) sono (mio) magliette, (questo) sono (tuo).
8 (Quello) esercizi sono (divertente), ma (questo) è (difficile).
9 (Mio) bagagli sono (pesante), ma (vostro) sono (leggero).
10 (Quello) acqua (minerale) è (gassato), ma (questo) è (liscio).

UNIT FOUR

The present tense of **essere** and **avere**

1 Like their counterparts in many other languages, the Italian verbs **essere** (to be) and **avere** (to have) are irregular. Here are the forms of the present tense:

Essere	*To be*	*Avere*	*To have*
(io) **sono**	I am	(io) **ho**	I have/have got
(tu) **sei**	you [sing.] are	(tu) **hai**	you [sing.] have/have got
(lui/lei) **è**	he/she/it is	(lui/lei) **ha**	he/she/it has/has got
(noi) **siamo**	we are	(noi) **abbiamo**	we have/have got
(voi) **siete**	you [pl.] are	(voi) **avete**	you [pl.] have/have got
(loro) **sono**	they are	(loro) **hanno**	they have/have got

Sono medico.	I'm a doctor.
Siamo cugini.	We are cousins.
Siete stranieri.	You are foreigners.
Paola e Anna sono alte.	Paola and Anna are tall.
Claudio è mio fratello.	Claudio is my brother.
Ho un cellulare.	I've got a mobile phone.
Hai il mio indirizzo.	You have my address.
Hanno un esame.	They have an exam.
Anna ha una chitarra nuova.	Anna's got a new guitar.

As shown in the examples, it is not usually necessary to use the subject pronouns before the verb since the forms for the different persons are different – **sei** can *only* be second person singular (**tu**), **siete** can *only* be second person plural (**voi**), etc. Even with **sono**, the context always shows whether it means 'I am' or 'they are'.

The pronoun is only required for emphasis, or to mark a contrast:

Io sono medico e lui è insegnante.	I'm a doctor and he's a teacher.
Tu hai una bella bici, ma io ho una macchina.	You've got a nice bike, but I've got a car.

Subject pronouns

2 The Italian subject pronouns are:

Person	Singular	
1st	**io**	I
2nd	**tu**	you
3rd	**lui**	he
3rd	**lei**	she
	Plural	
1st	**noi**	we
2nd	**voi**	you
3rd	**loro**	they

For the third person, the following pronouns can still be found in some texts, but are not normally used in contemporary Italian:

egli [m], **esso** [m]	instead of the singular **lui**
ella [f], **essa** [f]	instead of the singular **lei**
essi [m], **esse** [f]	instead of the plural **loro**

Lui (third person singular pronoun) replaces a masculine noun (like the English 'he'); **lei** replaces a feminine noun (like the English 'she').

Lui, **lei** and **loro** are only used to refer to persons. In referring to objects, Italian normally avoids using the obsolete forms **esso**, **essa**, **essi**, **esse**, and omits the pronoun altogether:

Lui è Paolo, lei è Anna.	He is Paolo, she is Anna.
'Cos'è?' 'È una chiave.'	'What is it?' 'It's a key.'
È la chitarra di Anna.	It's Anna's guitar.
Sono i libri di Paolo.	They are Paolo's books.

Interrogative form

3 The interrogative is formed by adding a question mark at the end of the sentence:

Sei pronto?	Are you ready?
Siete stranieri?	Are you foreigners?
Hai il mio indirizzo?	Have you got my address?
Avete amici italiani?	Have you any Italian friends?
Hanno un esame?	Have they got an exam?

Negative form

4 The negative is formed by putting **non** (i.e. 'not') before the verb:

Claudio non è mio fratello.	Claudio is not my brother.
Non siamo italiani.	We're not Italian.
Non siete stranieri?	Aren't you foreigners?
Non hai il mio indirizzo?	Haven't you got my address?
Non hanno un esame.	They don't have an exam.
Non abbiamo amici italiani.	We haven't got any Italian friends.
Non ho la minima idea di cosa regalare a Paola.	I haven't the slightest idea what to give Paola.

Formal form

5 In Italian there is a formal way of addressing people which is used with people we do not know, or when some degree of formality is required. When the formal form is required, the pronoun used for the singular, for both men and women, is **Lei** (third person singular); the pronoun used for the plural is normally **Voi**, but in situations when a high degree of formality is required **Loro** can be used:

Lei è molto gentile, Signore.	You're very kind(, Sir).
Lei non è troppo alta, Signora!	You're not too tall(, Madam)!
Signora Belli, (Lei) ha la patente?	Mrs Belli, have you got a driving licence?
Professore, (Lei) ha tempo?	Have you got time(, Professor/Sir)?
Signor Neri, (Lei) è pronto?	Mr Neri, are you ready?
Signori Conti, (Voi) siete italiani? **(Signori Conti, Loro sono italiani?)**	Mr and Mrs Conti, are you Italian?

6 There are some spelling mistakes involving **essere** and **avere** which are commonly made by learners; be careful to remember the following differences:

è (he/she/it is)	**e** (and)
ho (I have)	**o** (or)
hai (you have)	**ai** (to the)
ha (he/she/it has)	**a** (to)
hanno (they have)	**anno** (year)

Use of *essere* and *avere*

7 The verbs **essere** and **avere** are normally used as the verbs 'to be' and 'to have' are used in English. **Essere** is usually followed by an adjective or a noun:

Siete studenti? [noun]	Are you students? [noun]
Daniela è medico. [noun]	Daniela is a doctor. [noun]
Tu e Anna siete cugini? [noun]	Are you and Anna cousins? [noun]
Siete gentili! [adjective]	You are kind! [adjective]
Gli amici di Paul sono italiani. [adjective]	Paul's friends are Italian. [adjective]

Avere is normally followed by a noun (or a noun accompanied by an adjective):

Hai il libro?	Have you got the book?
Non ho tempo.	I haven't time.
Abbiamo molti amici.	We have a lot of friends.
Hanno una casa grande.	They have a big house.
Paolo e io abbiamo una macchina.	Paolo and I have got a car.

8 The verb **avere**, followed by a noun, is also used in a number of idiomatic expressions which correspond to English expressions using 'to be' followed by an adjective or an adverbial phrase:

avere caldo	to be hot
avere fame	to be hungry
avere freddo	to be cold
avere paura	to be afraid
avere ragione	to be right
avere sete	to be thirsty
avere sonno	to be sleepy
avere torto	to be wrong
avere fretta	to be in a hurry

Abbiamo fame.	We are hungry.
Avete ragione!	You're right!
Marina ha fretta.	Marina is in a hurry.
(Lei) ha sete, Signora?	Are you thirsty(, Madam)?
Non hai freddo, Claudia?	Aren't you cold, Claudia?

9 **Avere** is also used in Italian to express age:

Francesca ha 17 anni.	Francesca is 17 (years old).
Il figlio di Gianni ha un anno.	Gianni's son is one.
Quanti anni hai?	How old are you?

C'è and *ci sono*

10 The verb **essere** is used in the expressions **c'è** (there is) followed by a singular noun, and **ci sono** (there are) followed by a plural noun:

C'è una lettera per te.	There's a letter for you.
C'è poco tempo.	There's little/not much time.
C'è molto tempo!	There's plenty of time!
C'è un problema.	There's a problem.
Ci sono due ingressi.	There are two entrances.
Nel negozio ci sono molti clienti.	There are a lot of customers in the shop.

11 Note that **c'è** and **ci sono** are not usually emphatic. So, in the English sentences in paragraph 10, the voice stress does not fall on 'there', but on the noun that follows it (i.e. on 'letter', 'little/plenty of time', 'problem', etc.). Thus **c'è** and **ci sono** sometimes do not correspond to 'there is' or 'there are', as in the following examples:

C'è Luisa al telefono. [i.e. she has just rung]	Luisa's on the phone. [not: There's Luisa on the phone.]
Ci sono i tuoi amici che ti aspettano. [i.e. they have just arrived]	Your friends are waiting for you. [not: There are your friends waiting for you.]

12 The interrogative is formed by simply adding a question mark at the end of the sentence, or with a 'question word' (see Unit 9):

C'è il Professor Gatti?	Is Professor Gatti there/anywhere/around? [i.e. I'd like to see/talk to Professor Gatti.]
C'è molto traffico?	Is there a lot of traffic?
Quanti ingressi ci sono?	How many entrances are there?

13 The negative is formed by placing **non** before **c'è** or **ci sono**:

Non c'è tempo.	There is no time.
Domani non c'è lezione.	There is no class tomorrow.
Non ci sono clienti.	There aren't any customers.

Non c'è tempo?	Is there no time?
Non ci sono clienti?	Aren't there any customers?
Non c'è nessuno.*	There is nobody.*

* In Italian the double negative is used: **non + nessuno**.

14 Note that in negative sentences giving general information, it is more usual to use the plural **non ci sono** than the singular **non c'è**:

Non ci sono farmacie.	⎰ There isn't a/is no pharmacy. ⎱ There aren't any/are no pharmacies.
Non ci sono scuole.	⎰ There isn't a/is no school. ⎱ There aren't any/are no schools.
Non ci sono artisti nella mia famiglia.	There aren't any/are no artists in my family.

Exercise 1

Complete the following sentences using the correct form of **essere**.

Example: Alberto _____ a Roma: è

1 (noi) _____ italiani.
2 (tu) _____ scozzese?
3 (io) non _____ felice.
4 Gli studenti _____ in biblioteca.
5 (voi) _____ molto gentili.
6 Lei _____ medico?
7 La cena _____ pronta.
8 I libri _____ sulla scrivania.
9 Tu e Jim _____ amici.
10 Paolo e io _____ giovani.
11 Gli impiegati _____ gentili.
12 (voi) _____ simpatici.
13 Enrico non _____ biondo.
14 Gli italiani _____ allegri.
15 (tu) _____ amica di Giulia?
16 Laura _____ magra.
17 L'esercizio _____ difficile.
18 (io) _____ straniero.
19 Tu e Billy _____ stranieri.
20 (Lei) _____ stanca, Signora?

Exercise 2

Complete the following sentences using the correct form of **avere**.

Example: Jenny e John _____ una figlia: hanno

1 (noi) non _____ tempo.
2 (Lei) _____ la macchina?
3 (io) _____ molti amici.
4 I Signori Illy _____ due figli.
5 (voi) _____ i libri?
6 Sandro _____ sempre fretta.

7 Il professore _____ molti studenti.

8 (tu) _____ il libro?

9 Marco e io _____ sete.

10 Quanti anni (tu) _____?

11 (voi) _____ il biglietto?

12 Domenico _____ un fratello.

13 (noi) _____ un esame.

14 (loro) non _____ figli.

15 (tu) _____ l'indirizzo di Luca?

16 Carlo non _____ la televisione.

17 I nostri amici _____ dei problemi.

18 (tu) _____ molto lavoro.

19 (io) _____ 16 anni.

20 Professore, _____ tempo?

Exercise 3

Taking the words in the two columns below, write negative and interrogative sentences using the verb **avere**.

Example: tu   fretta: Non hai fretta; Hai fretta?

1 io   ragione
2 il professore   caldo
3 la Signorina Berti   sete
4 Lei [formal]   sonno
5 voi   paura
6 loro   freddo
7 Carla e Andrea   fame

Exercise 4

Taking the words in the two columns below, write affirmative and negative sentences using the verb **essere**.

Example: io   italiana: Sono italiana; Non sono italiana.

1 io   stanco
2 tu   pigra
3 il dottore   giovane
4 la professoressa   simpatica
5 Lei [formal]   alto
6 noi   magre
7 voi   intelligenti
8 le tue amiche   contente

Exercise 5

Imagine the things in the office; using all the words in the list, write sentences using **c'è** or **ci sono**.

> Examples: una scrivania: Nell'ufficio c'è una scrivania; quattro sedie:
>   Nell'ufficio ci sono quattro sedie.

1 una sedia; 2 due poltrone; 3 tre computer; 4 una stampante; 5 un telefono; 6 la fotocopiatrice; 7 due radiatori; 8 una porta; 9 tre finestre

Exercise 6

Imagine what is in the village; using all the words in the list, make affirmative or negative sentences, paying attention to the negative form (**non ci sono +** plural noun).

> Example: tabaccaio, tabaccai: In questo paese c'è un tabaccaio, ci sono
>   tre tabaccai, non ci sono tabaccai.

1 museo, musei; 2 discoteca, discoteche; 3 panetteria, panetterie; 4 cinema, cinema; 5 biblioteca, biblioteche; 6 scuola, scuole; 7 ufficio postale, uffici postali; 8 libreria, librerie; 9 giardino pubblico, giardini pubblici; 10 ristorante, ristoranti

UNIT FIVE

The present tense of regular (and some irregular) verbs

Use of the present tense

1 The present tense (or simply 'the present') is used to state that an action is occurring at the present time. It corresponds basically to the English simple present ('I eat') and present continuous ('I am eating'):

Mio padre lavora per la BBC.	My father works for the BBC.
Mio padre lavora in giardino.	My father's working in the garden.
Di solito guardo la televisione.	Normally I watch TV.
Stasera guardo la televisione.	I'm watching TV this evening.
Non guardo la televisione.	I don't watch TV.
Perché non guardi la televisione?	Why don't you watch TV?
Stasera non guardo la televisione.	I'm not watching TV this evening.
Perché non guardi la televisione stasera?	Why aren't you watching TV this evening?

2 The present can also be used to refer to the future, either the near future or one that is considered fairly certain:

Il treno parte fra cinque minuti.	The train leaves/is leaving in five minutes.
Parto domani.	I leave/I am leaving tomorrow.
Domani mattina porto Luca alla stazione.	Tomorrow morning I'll take/I'm taking/- I'm going to take Luca to the station.
L'estate prossima lavoro con mio zio.	Next summer I'll work/I'm working/- going to work with my uncle.

3 The present is also used to refer to an action which started in the past and is still going on; here, it corresponds to the English present perfect:

Lavoriamo qui da un mese.	We've been working here for a month.

Mio cugino abita a Roma da tre anni.	My cousin's lived/been living in Rome for three years.
Conosco Giulia da tre anni.	I have known Giulia for three years.
Non vedo Dario da mesi.	I haven't seen Dario for months.

The forms of the present tense

4 Italian verbs are divided into three main groups, the conjugations. The conjugation a verb belongs to is determined by the ending of its infinitive:

First conjugation	*Second conjugation*	*Third conjugation*
-are	**-ere**	**-ire**

The forms of the present depend on which conjugation the verb belongs to. The present is formed by changing the ending of the infinitive, as follows:

Person	*Singular*	*Infinitive in* **-are**	*Infinitive in* **-ere**	*Infinitive in* **-ire**
1st	(io)	**-o**	**-o**	**(-isc)-o**
2nd	(tu)	**-i**	**-i**	**(-isc)-i**
3rd	(lui/lei)	**-a**	**-e**	**(-isc)-e**
	Plural			
1st	(noi)	**-iamo**	**-iamo**	**-iamo**
2nd	(voi)	**-ate**	**-ete**	**-ite**
3rd	(loro)	**-ano**	**-ono**	**(-isc)-ono**

5 Regular verbs in **-are** are conjugated as follows:

Endings	*Parlare*	*To speak/talk*
-o	(io) **parlo**	I speak
-i	(tu) **parli**	you speak
-a	(lui/lei) **parla**	he/she/it speaks
-iamo	(noi) **parliamo**	we speak
-ate	(voi) **parlate**	you speak
-ano	(loro) **parlano**	they speak

Andrea e Carla lavorano in Italia.	Andrea and Carla work in Italy.
Parlo italiano.*	I speak Italian.
Parlate molto!*	You talk a lot!
Abitiamo a Genova.*	We live in Genoa.

* As we saw in Unit 4, the subject pronoun is normally omitted in the conjugation of Italian verbs.

6 Verbs ending in **-care** and **-gare** (first conjugation) add **h** before the endings of the second person singular (**-i**) and the first person plural (**-iamo**) in order to keep the hard sound of **c** and **g**:

Cercare	*To look for*	*Pagare*	*To pay*
(io) **cerco**	I look for	(io) **pago**	I pay
(tu) **cer*chi***	you look for	(tu) **pa*ghi***	you pay
(lui/lei) **cerca**	he/she/it looks for	(lui/lei) **paga**	he/she/it pays
(noi) **cer*chi*amo**	we look for	(noi) **pa*ghi*amo**	we pay
(voi) **cercate**	you look for	(voi) **pagate**	you pay
(loro) **cercano**	they look for	(loro) **pagano**	they pay

Cerchi Marco?	Are you looking for Marco?
Giochiamo a pallone.	We play football.
Perché litighi con tuo fratello?	Why are you arguing with your brother?
Paghiamo sempre il conto!	We always pay the bill!

7 Verbs ending in **-iare** (first conjugation) normally have only one **i** in the second person singular and the first person plural:

Cominciare	*To start/begin*	*Mangiare*	*To eat*
(io) **comincio**	I start/begin	(io) **mangio**	I eat
(tu) **cominc*i***	you start/begin	(tu) **mang*i***	you eat
(lui/lei) **comincia**	he/she/it starts/begins	(lui/lei) **mangia**	he/she/it eats
(noi) **cominc*iamo***	we start/begin	(noi) **mang*iamo***	we eat
(voi) **cominciate**	you start/begin	(voi) **mangiate**	you eat
(loro) **cominciano**	they start/begin	(loro) **mangiano**	they eat

Quando cominci la scuola?	When do you start school?
Cominciamo la partita.	We're starting the game.
Mangi troppo!	You eat too much!
Stasera mangiamo fuori.	This evening we're eating out.

8 Regular verbs in **-ere** are conjugated as follows:

Endings	*Prendere*	*To take/get*
-o	(io) **prend*o***	I take/get
-i	(tu) **prend*i***	you take/get
-e	(lui/lei) **prend*e***	he/she/it takes/gets
-iamo	(noi) **prend*iamo***	we take/get
-ete	(voi) **prend*ete***	you take/get
-ono	(loro) **prend*ono***	they take/get

Prendo il prossimo treno.	I'm getting/taking the next train.
Prendiamo questa strada.	We take this road.
Anna scrive una lettera.	Anna is writing a letter.
Marco e Martina ridono molto.	Marco and Martina laugh a lot.

9 Verbs ending in **-cere** (or **-scere**) and **-gere** (or **-ggere**) change the sound of **c** (or **sc**) and **g** (or **-gg**), which become 'hard' before the endings of the first person singular (**-o**) and the third person plural (**-ono**). So care needs to be taken in speaking these verbs:

Vincere	*Spoken like English*	*To win*
(io) **vinco**	k	I win
(tu) **vinci**	ch	you win
(lui/lei) **vince**	ch	he/she/it wins
(noi) **vinciamo**	ch	we win
(voi) **vincete**	ch	you win
(loro) **vincono**	k	they win

Conoscere	*Spoken like English*	*To know*
(io) **conosco**	sk	I know
(tu) **conosci**	sh	you know
(lui/lei) **conosce**	sh	he/she/it knows
(noi) **conosciamo**	sh	we know
(voi) **conoscete**	sh	you know
(loro) **conoscono**	sk	they know

Leggere	*Spoken like English*	*To read*
(io) **leggo**	g [as in 'go']	I read
(tu) **leggi**	j	you read
(lui/lei) **legge**	j	he/she/it reads
(noi) **leggiamo**	j	we read
(voi) **leggete**	j	you read
(loro) **leggono**	g [as in 'go']	they read

Vince sempre.	He/she always wins.
Non conosco i tuoi genitori.	I don't know your parents.
Leggono il giornale.	They're reading the paper.
Non piango mai.	I never cry.

10 Regular verbs in **-ire** are conjugated as follows:

Endings	Partire	To leave
-o	(io) **part***o*	I leave
-i	(tu) **part***i*	you leave
-e	(lui/lei) **part***e*	he/she/it leaves
-iamo	(noi) **part***iamo*	we leave
-ite	(voi) **part***ite*	you leave
-ono	(loro) **part***ono*	they leave

Il treno parte alle 8.00. The train leaves at eight.
I miei amici partono domani. My friends are leaving tomorrow.
Mia sorella dorme. My sister is sleeping/asleep.
Tutte le mattine apriamo le finestre. Every morning we open the windows.

11 Many verbs in **-ire** (e.g. **capire** (to understand), **costruire** (to build), **finire** (to finish/to end), **preferire** (to prefer), **pulire** (to clean)) follow a slightly different pattern, adding **-isc-** before the singular endings and the third person plural:

Endings	Capire	To understand
-isc-o	(io) **cap***isco*	I understand
-isc-i	(tu) **cap***isci*	you understand
-isc-e	(lui/lei) **cap***isce*	he/she/it understands
-iamo	(noi) **cap***iamo*	we understand
-ite	(voi) **cap***ite*	you understand
-isc-ono	(loro) **cap***iscono*	they understand

Marina capisce tutto. Marina understands everything.
La lezione finisce alle 13.00. The lesson/class finishes at 1 p.m.
Preferisco parlare italiano. I prefer speaking/to speak Italian.

There is no way of telling which is the right pattern for a verb in **-ire**, other than to check in a dictionary.

Interrogative form

12 As we saw in Unit 4, the interrogative is formed by adding a question mark at the end of the sentence:

Carla resta a casa? Is Carla staying at home?
Prendi sempre la macchina fotografica? Do you always take the camera?
Quando partite? When are you leaving?
Capisci tutto? Do you understand everything?

Negative form

13 The negative is formed by putting **non** (not) before the verb:

Non parlo italiano.	I don't speak Italian.
Non prendiamo la macchina fotografica.	We're not taking the camera.
Giulia e Susanna non partono?	Aren't Giulia and Susanna leaving?
Non capisce niente.	He/she doesn't understand anything.

Formal form

14 As we saw in Unit 4, the pronouns used for the formal form are **Lei** for the singular (for both women and men) and **Voi** for the plural (the pronoun **Loro** is much more formal):

(Lei) Parla italiano?	Do you speak Italian?
Non prende un taxi, Professor Masi?	Aren't you taking a taxi, Professor Masi?
Partite, Signori Bianco? ⎱ **((Loro) Partono, Signori Bianco?)** ⎰	Are you leaving(, Mr and Mrs Bianco)?

Present tense of some irregular verbs

15 In Italian, as in most languages, there are a number of irregular verbs whose conjugation is best learned by heart and with use. Here is the conjugation of some of the more frequently used irregular verbs:

Dare (to give)	*Stare* (to stay/live/feel)	*Sapere* (to know)
dò	sto	so
dai	stai	sai
dà	sta	sa
diamo	stiamo	sappiamo
date	state	sapete
danno	stanno	sanno

Andare (to go)	*Uscire* (to go out/leave)	*Venire* (to come)
vado	esco	vengo
vai	esci	vieni
va	esce	viene
andiamo	usciamo	veniamo
andate	uscite	venite
vanno	escono	vengono

Dovere (must/to have to)	*Potere* (can/may/to be able)	*Volere* (to wish/to want)
devo	posso	voglio
devi	puoi	vuoi
deve	può	vuole
dobbiamo	possiamo	vogliamo
dovete	potete	volete
devono	possono	vogliono

Dire (to say/tell)	*Fare* (to do/make)	*Bere* (to drink)
dico	faccio	bevo
dici	fai	bevi
dice	fa	beve
diciamo	facciamo	beviamo
dite	fate	bevete
dicono	fanno	bevono

The verb **riuscire** (to succeed/manage/be able to) follows the same pattern as **uscire**.

Cosa fai?	What are you doing?
'Come stai?' 'Sto bene, grazie.'	'How are you?' 'I'm fine, thank you.'
Mia zia sta a Bologna.	My aunt lives in Bologna.
Vado al cinema.	I'm going to the cinema.
Stasera non esco.	I'm not going out tonight.
Domani esco presto.	I'm leaving early tomorrow.
Non riesco a capire.	I can't understand.
Non riesco a chiudere la porta.	I can't manage to close the door.
Adesso sapete tutto.	Now you know everything.*

* It is important not to confuse **sapere** and **conoscere** (paragraph 9). Both mean 'to know', but they are not always interchangeable. The basic difference is that **sapere** generally means 'to know/be aware of/to have knowledge of *a fact*' (but see also paragraph 17 below), whereas **conoscere** means 'to be acquainted/familiar with', or sometimes 'to meet/make the acquaintance of' (e.g. in the expression **piacere di conoscerti**, pleased to meet you). Thus **sapere** is never used for people, and **conoscere** is never followed by a phrase containing a verb:

Sappiamo già che c'è sciopero domani.	We already know that there is a strike tomorrow.
Sai che ora è?	Do you know what time it is?
Sai perché?	Do you know why?
Non so che cosa fare.	I don't know what to do.
Conosco le regole del gioco.	I know the rules of the game.

Ho conosciuto il padre di Pia.	I (have) met Pia's father.
Non conosco il tuo ragazzo.	I don't know your boyfriend.
Conosci questa città?	Do you know this town?

16 **Dovere**, **potere** and **volere** usually need to be followed by another verb in the infinitive:

Dobbiamo fare gli esercizi.	We've got to do the exercises.
Posso parlare con Luigi?	May I talk to Luigi?
Puoi telefonare domani.	You can phone tomorrow.
Non vogliono uscire.	They don't want to go out.

17 The verb **sapere** is another that is often followed by a verb in the infinitive; used in this way, it expresses the ability to do something (in the sense of 'to know how to' do something):

So nuotare.	I can swim. [i.e. I know how to]
Paolo non sa ballare.	Paolo can't dance. [i.e. he doesn't know how to]
Sai usare quello scanner?	Can you/Do you know how to use that scanner?

18 A few verbs end in **-urre** (like **condurre** (to lead/drive/manage), **tradurre** (to translate), **produrre** (to produce), etc.); all have the following pattern:

Endings	Produrre	To produce
-uc-o	(io) prod**uc**o	I produce
-uc-i	(tu) prod**uc**i	you produce
-uc-e	(lui/lei) prod**uc**e	he/she/it produces
-uc-iamo	(noi) prod**uc**iamo	we produce
-uc-ete	(voi) prod**uc**ete	you produce
-uc-ono	(loro) prod**uc**ono	they produce

Questa fabbrica produce automobili.	This factory produces cars.
Traducono dal francese.	They translate from French.

Exercise 1

Supply the present tense of the verb in brackets.

Example: Non (io conoscere) tua mamma: conosco

1 Claudio (arrivare) con il prossimo treno.
2 Anna (vivere) a Roma.
3 Non (noi mangiare) spesso fuori.
4 (tu cercare) casa?
5 Stasera (voi prendere) l'autobus.

6   Il treno di Giorgio (partire) alle 18.
7   Tutti i giorni (noi leggere) il giornale.
8   (tu pulire) il bagno?
9   (io conoscere) molti italiani.
10 I giochi (finire) sempre alle 17.
11 Non (noi guidare) l'auto.
12 Anna e io (giocare) a carte.
13 Perché non (voi tornare) in Scozia?
14 Non (tu capire) nulla!
15 Giorgio e Paola non (spendere) molto.
16 Dove (Lei abitare), Signor Verdi?
17 (Voi pagare) l'affitto, Signori Rossi?
18 (tu viaggiare) molto.
19 Non (tu ricevere) molte lettere?
20 Piero e Gianni (lasciare) il cane a casa.

Exercise 2

Supply the present tense of the verb in brackets.

Example: (io bere) molta acqua: bevo

1   Stasera (loro) andare al cinema.
2   La nostra fabbrica (produrre) pasta.
3   Domani (noi dare) una festa.
4   (tu andare) spesso in spiaggia?
5   (voi fare) gli esercizi?
6   Non (noi riuscire) a capire.
7   (voi venire) a casa?
8   Non (io potere) uscire oggi.
9   (loro volere) dormire.
10 (tu dire) la verità?
11 Tu e Claudia (potere) partire.
12 (io volere) studiare.
13 Dove (tu stare) adesso?
14 Le mie sorelle non (sapere) nuotare.
15 Cosa (loro fare) stasera?
16 I vicini (dovere) rimanere a casa.
17 (noi tradurre) in italiano.
18 Luigi (dovere) lavorare.
19 (voi sapere) cantare?
20 I nostri amici (venire) a Roma.

Exercise 3

Translate into Italian:

1   You [pl.] have got to talk to Marcello.
2   We're leaving tonight.
3   We're getting the next bus.
4   You [polite] can go to the cinema, Mr Buchan.
5   We know how to use those mobile phones.
6   She always prefers reading the paper.
7   The baby's asleep.
8   I'm coming to Turin this summer.

9 They often go out in the evening.
10 The boys are playing football tomorrow.

Exercise 4

Translate into Italian:

1 Are you going out tonight, Mother?
2 What are we doing tomorrow?
3 Can you [sing.] open that door?
4 Do you [sing.] want a coffee?
5 Can you play the piano, Francesco?
6 What are you [sing.] looking for?
7 Are you [polite] drinking coffee or mineral water, Madam?
8 Do you [sing.] and Jim know my parents?
9 Are you [sing.] well today?
10 What are they building?

Exercise 5

Translate into Italian:

1 Don't you [polite] speak English, Mrs Vialli?
2 My German friends can't sing in Italian.
3 I don't earn a lot.
4 Isn't she giving a party for her birthday?
5 Aren't you [sing.] working with Giulia?
6 They've not seen Mr Moro for three years.
7 Why do you never go to Florence, Claudio?
8 I can't manage to shut this window.
9 Why aren't you [pl.] drinking coffee this morning?
10 Aren't you [pl.] coming tomorrow?

UNIT SIX
Adverbs

1 English adverbs are usually formed by adding '-ly' to an adjective (e.g. 'thin*ly*', 'clever*ly*'). Italian adverbs are usually just as easy to form: **-mente** is added to the feminine singular form of the adjective:

lent*a* + -mente	**lentamente**	slowly
rapid*a* + -mente	**rapidamente**	quickly
semplic*e* + -mente	**semplicemente**	simply
frequent*e* + -mente	**frequentemente**	frequently

When the adjective ends in **-le** or **-re** preceded by a vowel, the final **e** is dropped before adding **-mente**:

gent*ile* + -mente	**gentilmente**	kindly, politely
ut*ile* + -mente	**utilmente**	usefully
maggi*ore* + -mente	**maggiormente**	mainly
regol*are* + -mente	**regolarmente**	regularly

Il tempo cambia *rapidamente*.	The weather changes quickly.
La nonna cammina *lentamente*.	Granny walks slowly.
Enrico risponde sempre *gentilmente*.	Enrico always answers politely.
Faccio i compiti *regolarmente*.	I do my homework regularly.

2 In Italian there are also many adverbs which do not end in **-mente**. Here are some:

abbastanza	enough/fairly/rather/ quite	**forte**	loudly/hard
		fuori	out/outside
ancora	still	**già**	already
bene	well	**lontano**	far (away)
davanti	at the front/in front	**male**	badly
dentro	in(side)	**non . . . ancora**	not yet
dietro	at the back/behind	**non . . . mai**	never
dopo	later/afterwards	**piano**	slowly/quietly

più	more	**sopra**	above/upstairs
piuttosto	rather	**sotto**	below/downstairs
presto	soon/early	**spesso**	often
prima	earlier/beforehand/ first	**subito**	immediately/right away
		tardi	late
quasi	almost	**vicino**	near(by)
sempre	always	**volentieri**	willingly/gladly

Questo film è *abbastanza* bello.	This film is rather good.
Partiamo *tardi*: dopo le 11.	We're leaving late: after 11.
Andiamo *spesso* in discoteca.	We often go to the disco.
Vengo *subito*!	I'm coming (immediately)!
Parto *presto*.	I'm leaving early/soon.
Parliamo *piano* perchè Carla dorme.	We're talking quietly because Carla's asleep.
Può parlare *piano*, per favore? Non sono italiano.	Could you speak slowly, please? I'm not Italian.
Abita *vicino*, Signora?	Do you live nearby (Madam)?
Vai *lontano*?	Are you going far?
Piove *forte*.	It's raining hard.
Puoi parlare *più forte*?	Can you speak louder/more loudly?
Mangiamo *fuori*.	We're eating out [e.g. in a restaurant]/ outside [i.e. in the open].
È *ancora* estate.	It's still summer.
Non* è *ancora* estate.	It's not summer yet.
Non* esco *mai*.	I never go out.
Lorenzo *non* telefona *mai*.*	Lorenzo never phones.

* Note that with **non . . . ancora** and **non . . . mai**, **non** is always placed before the verb and **ancora**/mai after it.

3 Adverbs can qualify verbs, adjectives or even other adverbs:

Dormo bene. [verb + adverb]	I sleep well.
Dormo molto bene. [adverb + adverb]	I sleep very well.
La casa è molto piccola. [adverb + adjective]	The house is very small.

4 Some words denoting quantity can be used both as adverbs and as adjectives: **molto/tanto** (a lot (of)/very/many), **troppo** (too much/too many) and **poco** (few/little/not much/not very). When used as *adverbs* they are invariable, but when used as *adjectives* they agree in gender and number with the noun they refer to:

Adverb

lavorare molto/tanto	to work a lot
molto/tanto lontano	very far
molto/tanto difficile	very difficult
lavorare troppo	to work too much
troppo lontano	too far
troppo difficile	too difficult
lavorare poco	to work little/not to work much
poco lontano	not very far
poco difficile	not very difficult

Adjective

molto (tanto)/troppo/poco lavoro [ms]	a lot of/too much/not much work
molta (tanta)/troppa/poca acqua [fs]	a lot of/too much/not much water
molti (tanti)/troppi/pochi esercizi [mp]	many/too many/not many exercises
molte (tante)/troppe/poche lettere [fp]	many/too many/not many letters

Mio padre lavora *troppo*. [adverb]	My father works too much.
Questa musica è *molto* bella. [adverb]	This music is very beautiful.
Luisa dorme *poco*. [adverb]	Luisa sleeps little/doesn't sleep much.
Dormi *troppo poco*. [adverbs]	You sleep too little/don't sleep enough.
Abbiamo *molto* tempo. [adjective]	We have a lot of time.
Luisa mangia *poca* pasta. [adjective]	Luisa eats little pasta/doesn't eat a lot of pasta.
Ho *molti* amici. [adjective]	I have a lot of friends.
'Perché fai questo?' 'Ci sono *molte* ragioni.' [adjective]	'Why are you doing this?' 'There are many reasons.'

Adverbial expressions

5 Having a lot of words ending in **-mente** can often sound heavy. To avoid this, Italian sometimes uses adverbial phrases instead of single words. These do the same job as one-word adverbs, and indeed they do usually correspond to one-word English adverbs in '-ly'. These adverbial expressions are most often constructed with **con** (with), sometimes with **senza** (without), followed by a noun:

con difficoltà	with difficulty
con eleganza	elegantly
con lentezza	slowly
con rapidità	rapidly/quickly
con semplicità	simply

senza eleganza	inelegantly
senza complicazioni	uncomplicatedly
senza dubbio	undoubtedly

There are also a number of adverbial expressions that use other prepositions than **con**. Here are some of the most common:

a poco a poco	little by little
a volte	sometimes
in ritardo	late
in tempo	on time
di solito	usually
di sicuro	surely/certainly

Anna veste *con eleganza*.	Anna dresses elegantly.
Spieghi tutto *senza complicazioni*.	You explain everything uncomplicatedly.
A volte **non capisco quello che dice.**	Sometimes I don't understand what he says.

Another adverbial expression that is sometimes used is **in modo/in maniera** (i.e. 'in a way') followed by an adjective; the adjective is masculine when used with **modo** and feminine when used with **maniera**:

in modo vago/in maniera vaga	vaguely/in a vague way
in modo strano/in maniera strana	strangely/in a strange way
in modo semplice/in maniera semplice	simply/in a simple way

Risponde sempre in modo vago.	He/she always answers vaguely.
Quel cane cammina in maniera strana.	That dog's walking oddly/in a strange way.

Exercise 1

Change the adjectives into adverbs.

Example: lento: lentamente

1	dolce	6	irregolare	11	lento
2	tranquillo	7	probabile	12	utile
3	semplice	8	chiaro	13	attento
4	allegro	9	facile	14	rapido
5	maggiore	10	veloce	15	leggero

Exercise 2

Supply the correct form of **molto/tanto**, **troppo** or **poco** (adverbs or adjectives).

Examples: Anna è (molto) alta: molto; Ho (molto) sete: molta

1   Claudia mangia (molto) dolci.
2   Il tuo vestito è (molto) bello.
3   Monica ha (poco) amici.
4   Tu spendi (troppo).
5   In mensa ci sono (troppo) studenti.
6   Davanti al cinema c'è (tanto) gente.
7   Mangi (troppo)!
8   Stefano abita (molto) lontano.
9   Giulia mangia sempre (poco).
10 Judy ha (molto) amiche italiane.
11 Sto (poco) bene.
12 Abitate in una casa (molto) bella.
13 Signora, è (molto) stanca?
14 Ci sono (poco) biscotti.
15 Siete (molto) gentili!
16 Hai (poco) pazienza.
17 Marco e Luisa hanno (molto) fame.
18 Il giardino non è (molto) grande.
19 Non devi invitare (troppo) persone.
20 Abbiamo (poco) riviste.

Exercise 3

Replace the words in English with the appropriate expression from the list:

a volte, di sicuro, con pazienza, senza esitazione, in modo nervoso, in tempo, con semplicità, di solito, con prudenza, a poco a poco, in maniera brusca, con coraggio

Examples: (sometimes) non voglio giocare a pallone: a volte; Laura veste (simply): con semplicità

1   Dobbiamo agire (cautiously).
2   Andrea spiega tutto (patiently).
3   Paolo guarda i professori (nervously).
4   (little by little) Gianni capisce il problema.
5   Tullio risponde (unhesitatingly).
6   (usually) rientra nel pomeriggio.
7   Lei non fa più (in time) a prendere il treno delle sette.
8   Esprime (courageously) le sue opinioni.
9   Domenica vengo (for sure).
10 Il Signor Capello risponde (bluntly) a tutte le nostre domande.

Exercise 4

Translate into Italian:

1 Sometimes I eat in the canteen.
2 The swimming pool is quite big.
3 We often go out with our friends.
4 Have you [sing.] got enough money?
5 You [sing.] have to speak slowly.
6 Marina never eats cheese.
7 Francesca always arrives late.
8 I've been waiting for almost forty minutes!
9 Carla and Andrea are out.
10 Are your [sing.] parents well?

UNIT SEVEN
Direct object pronouns (1)

1 A direct object is the person or thing that the verb directly impacts on: **Invito** *Elena* (I'm inviting *Elena*); **Uso** *il computer* **tutti i giorni** (I use *the computer* every day).

A direct object pronoun replaces a noun used as a direct object; it must therefore agree in gender and number with the noun it refers to. Direct object pronouns normally come before the verb. In the following examples, the pronouns are in italics:

Quando vedo Elena *la* **invito a cena.**	When I see Elena I'll invite
[*la* replaces and agrees with **Elena** (fs)]	*her* to dinner.
Quando vedo Lorenzo *lo* **invito a cena.**	When I see Lorenzo I'll invite
[*lo* replaces and agrees with **Lorenzo** (ms)]	*him* to dinner.
Scrivo le cartoline e poi *le* **imbuco.**	I write the postcards and
[*le* replaces and agrees with **le cartoline** (fp)]	then post *them*.
Appena compro i biscotti *li* **mangio.**	As soon as I buy biscuits I
[*li* replaces and agrees with **i biscotti** (mp)]	eat *them*.
Prendo il giornale e *lo* **leggo subito.**	I get the paper and read *it*
[*lo* replaces and agrees with **il giornale** (ms)]	immediately.

2 The forms of the direct object pronouns are as follows:

Subject	*Direct object*	
io	**mi**	me
tu	**ti**	you
lui/lei	**lo** [m]/**la** [f]	him/her/it
noi	**ci**	us
voi	**vi**	you
loro	**li** [m]/**le** [f]	them

Giacomo *mi* invita spesso a cena.	Giacomo often invites *me* to dinner.
Se vuoi, *ti* aiuto.	If you want, I'll help *you*.
Lo conosco bene.	I know *him* well.
La vedo tutti i giorni.	I see *her* every day.
Vi invito alla festa.	I'm inviting *you* to the party.

3 We saw in Unit 3 that if an adjective refers to two or more nouns that are different in gender, it has the masculine plural form, e.g. **Laura e Piero sono italian*i*** (Laura and Piero are Italian). The same principle applies to direct object pronouns:

'Conosci Laura [f] e Piero [m]?' 'Sì, *li* [mp] conosco bene.'	'Do you know Laura and Piero?' 'Yes. I know *them* well.'
'Usi il computer [m] e la stampante [f]?' 'Sì, *li* [mp] uso spesso.'	'Do you use the computer and the printer?' 'Yes, I often use *them*.'

Negative form

4 The negative is formed by putting **non** before the pronoun:

Non *lo* conosco bene.	I don't know him well.
Non *vi* invito alla festa.	I'm not inviting you to the party.
Non *li* vedo spesso.	I don't often see them.
Non *ti* capisco.	I don't understand you.

5 When a direct object pronoun is used with a verb in the infinitive (usually after verbs like **dovere**, **potere**, **volere** or **sapere**), it can be attached to the infinitive, which drops the final vowel:

La devo chiamare.	*or*	Devo chiamar*la*.	I must call her.
Ti voglio invitare.	*or*	Voglio invitar*ti*.	I want to invite you.
Lo puoi prendere.	*or*	Puoi prender*lo*.	You can take it.
Lo so fare.	*or*	So far*lo*.	I can/know how to do it.
Lo devo tradurre.*	*or*	Devo tradur*lo*.*	I've got to translate it.

Each pair of sentences has exactly the same meaning – the form used makes no difference.

* Note that verbs in **-urre** drop the second **r** as well as the final vowel: **lo devo tradurre** *or* **devo tradurlo**.

6 The pronoun **lo** [ms] is often used to replace a whole clause:

'Sai che oggi è il compleanno di Carla?' 'Sì, *lo* so.' [*lo* = oggi è il compleanno di Carla]	'Do you know that it's Carla's birthday today?' 'Yes, I do.' [lit. Yes, I know it]
'Dove sono le chiavi?' 'Non *lo* so.' [*lo* = dove sono le chiavi]	'Where are the keys?' 'I don't know.' [lit. I don't know it]
'Devi cambiare la cartuccia.' '*Lo* faccio subito.' [*lo* = cambiare la cartuccia]	'You've got to replace the cartridge.' 'I'll do it straight away.'

7 When the pronouns **lo** and **la** are used with the verb **avere**, they are shortened to **l'**, and are often preceded by the particle **ce**:

'Hai la cartuccia?' 'Sì, *ce l'*ho.'	'Have you got the cartridge?' 'Yes, I've got it.'
Non posso leggere il libro di Primo Levi perché non *ce l'*ho.	I can't read Primo Levi's book because I haven't got it.
'Avete l'indirizzo di Anna?' 'Sì, *ce l'*abbiamo.'	'Have you got Anna's address?' 'Yes, we have/Yes, we've got it.'

The plural pronouns **li** and **le**, however, are never shortened, and are only rarely used with **ce**:

'Hai le parole di questa canzone?' 'No, non (*ce*) *le* ho.'	'Have you got the lyrics of this song?' 'No, I haven't /No, I've not got them.'
'Hai i libri?' 'Sì, (*ce*) *li* ho.'	'Have you got the books?' 'Yes, I've got them/Yes, I have.'

Formal form

8 The direct object pronouns used for the formal form are **La** for the singular (for both women and men) and **Vi** for the plural (the pronouns **Li** and **Le** can also be used for the masculine and feminine respectively, but this is particularly formal):

Professor Masi, La accompagno in aeroporto.	Professor Masi, I'll take you to the airport.
Signora, La accompagno in aeroporto.	I'll take you to the airport, Madam.
Signori Bianco, Vi accompagno in aeroporto. **(Signori Bianco, Li accompagno in aeroporto.)**	Mr and Mrs Bianco, I'll take you to the airport.
Signore, Vi accompagno in aeroporto. **(Signore, Le accompagno in aeroporto.)**	(Ladies,) I'll take you to the airport.

Exercise 1

Rewrite the sentences, replacing the words in italics with the correct direct object pronoun.

Example: Luigi compra *il pane*: Luigi lo compra.

 1 Anna guarda *la televisione*.
 2 Invitiamo *i nostri amici*.
 3 Scrivete *le cartoline*?
 4 Leggono *il giornale*.
 5 Suono *la chitarra*.
 6 Preparo *la cena*.
 7 Chiamo *Roberto*.
 8 Faccio *gli esercizi*.
 9 Invito *Maria e Giovanna*.
10 Chiudete *le finestre*.
11 Lorenzo corregge *gli errori*.
12 Prendono *il treno*.
13 Porto *i CD*.
14 Cerco *i miei libri*.
15 Pia beve *l'acqua minerale*.
16 Paola finisce *il lavoro*.
17 Accompagno *Carlo e Anna*.
18 Vedi *le tue amiche* oggi?
19 Ascolto *la radio*.
20 Luca lava *i piatti*.

Exercise 2

Change the sentences into the negative.

Example: Lo faccio: Non lo faccio.

1 Le voglio.
2 Li compriamo.
3 Ci chiamano.
4 Silvia li invita?
5 I Signori Bianchi lo prendono.
6 Mi invitate?
7 Vi aspetto.
8 La vedo domani.
9 Ti accompagno alla stazione.
10 Lo guardiamo.

Exercise 3

Rewrite the sentences, changing the position of the pronoun.

Example: Li devi comprare: Devi comprarli.

1 Lo vogliamo vedere.
2 Non ti posso aiutare.
3 Mi puoi accompagnare?
4 La vuoi sentire?
5 Ci devono chiamare.
6 Vi voglio invitare.
7 Le vuole conoscere.
8 Non li potete fare.
9 Mi devi ascoltare.
10 Non La posso aiutare, Signora.

Exercise 4

Complete the sentences with the appropriate direct object pronouns.

> Examples: Marco telefona agli amici e _____ invita alla festa: li; Guido non
> sta bene: devo chiamar_____ : lo

1 Compro il giornale e _____ leggo.
2 Scrivo le cartoline e _____ spedisco.
3 Laura fa i panini e poi _____ mangia.
4 Compro i fiori e _____ metto in un vaso.
5 Apriamo la finestra e poi _____ chiudiamo.
6 Non riesco a fare questo esercizio: _____ aiuti?
7 Prendiamo i libri e _____ portiamo a scuola.
8 Professor Bartoli, _____ posso aiutare?
9 I Signori Pieri partono: _____ accompagni in aeroporto?
10 Hai molte amiche: _____ inviti tutte?
11 Se non usi la bici _____ prendo io.
12 Ci sono molti errori: _____ dovete correggere.
13 Claudio telefona a Giulia e _____ invita alla festa.
14 Partite? _____ porto in stazione.
15 C'è un film alla televisione ma non _____ guardiamo.
16 Alma parte: volete salutar_____?
17 La sorella di Matteo è molto simpatica. _____ conosco bene.
18 Gli esercizi sono difficili, ma _____ so fare.
19 Se vuoi delle caramelle, _____ puoi prendere.
20 'Sai che Alessandro suona il sassofono in un gruppo?' 'Sì, _____ so.'

Exercise 5

Translate into Italian:

1 We're inviting you [pl.] to the party.
2 I've got a lot of friends, and I often see them.
3 Signora Fusi, can I call you tomorrow?
4 Are you [sing.] helping us next week?
5 I have to see you [sing.].
6 Olga and Anna are leaving tomorrow and I want to take them to the
   station.
7 I can't help you [pl.].
8 'Are you [sing.] bringing the guitar?' 'No, I haven't got it.'
9 Tullio buys these magazines and reads them.
10 Can you [sing.] take me to school tomorrow?

UNIT EIGHT
Prepositions

1 The most common Italian prepositions are the following:

di	of
a	to
da	from
in	in
con	with
su	on
per	for
tra/fra*	among, between

* The meaning of **tra** and **fra** is the same.

These prepositions often correspond to the English counterparts we give here. However, as we shall see, each of them also has a number of other meanings, corresponding to other English prepositions.

2 The prepositions **di**, **a**, **da**, **in** and **su**, when used together with a noun preceded by the definite article, always combine with the article:

	il	*lo*	*l'*	*la*	*i*	*gli*	*le*
di	del	dello	dell'	della	dei	degli	delle
a	al	allo	all'	alla	ai	agli	alle
da	dal	dallo	dall'	dalla	dai	dagli	dalle
in	nel	nello	nell'	nella	nei	negli	nelle
su	sul	sullo	sull'	sulla	sui	sugli	sulle

The preposition **con** normally combines only with **il** and **i**, as **col** and **coi**; this form is common in spoken Italian, though **con il** and **con i** are often found in the written language:

con	con il	con lo	con l'	con la	con i	con gli	con le
	col	(collo)	(coll')	(colla)	coi	(cogli)	(colle)

di + *il* ragazzo	*del* ragazzo	of the boy
a + *lo* studente	*allo* studente	to the student
da + *l'*albergo	*dall'*albergo	from the hotel
in + *la* scuola	*nella* scuola	in the school
su + *i* divani	*sui* divani	on the sofas
con + *i* libri	*coi* libri	with the books
con + *le* chiavi	*con le* chiavi	with the keys
per + *gli* insegnanti	*per gli* insegnanti	for the teachers
fra + *i* calciatori	*fra i* calciatori	among the footballers

Using prepositions

3 As in many other languages, there is so much variation in how Italian prepositions are used that it is not feasible to give simple rules covering every possibility. To appreciate the problem, you only have to look at a few of the possible uses of the preposition **di**:

il presidente della repubblica	the president of the republic
Il libro è di Calvino.	The book is by Calvino.
Sono di Roma.	I'm from Rome.
Di pomeriggio fanno sempre la siesta.	They always have a nap in the afternoon.

Sometimes, Italian even has a preposition where English does not; here are some typical examples:

l'auto di Anna	Anna's car
Vuoi della frutta?	Do you want (some/any) fruit?
Ci sono alcune migliaia di persone nella piazza.	There are a few thousand people in the square.
Ho una bella camicia di seta.	I've got a lovely silk shirt.

Since there is not a simple set of rules governing prepositions in Italian, what we are going to do is show some typical uses of the common ones listed above. The more you hear and read Italian, the more you will encounter different uses of these and other prepositions; the best way of mastering them is to learn them and practise them as you go along.

4 **Di** is typically used to express:

possession	**La moto *di* Luca è rossa.**	Luca's motorbike is red.
material	**una giacca *di* pelle**	a leather jacket
time	**_Di_ sera non esco.**	I don't go out in the evening(s).
subject	**una lezione *di* storia**	a history lesson

The most common uses of **di** are the ones which correspond to the English possessive ('s) and the noun + noun structure:

il libro *del* professore	the teacher's book
la sorella *di* Monica	Monica's sister
il casco *di* Sebastiano	Sebastiano's helmet
la politica *del* governo	the government's policy/government policy
una buca *delle* lettere	a letter box
un racconto *di* fate	a fairy tale
il professore *di* scienze	the science teacher
un panino *di* formaggio	a cheese roll

Di is frequently used in partitive constructions, i.e. to express the English 'some' or 'any' in such sentences as 'I'd like some bread', 'Have you any pasta?', 'We've got (some) pasta and (some) olives':

Devo comprare *del* pane.	I've got to get (some) bread.
Prendo *della* pasta.	I'm getting (some) pasta.
C'è *dell'*acqua in frigo.	There's (some) water in the fridge.
Esco con *degli* amici.	I'm going out with (some) friends.
Vuoi *dei* libri in italiano?	Do you want (some) books in Italian?
Ci sono *delle* case sulla collina.	There are (some) houses on the hill.

Di is also used, followed by a verb in the infinitive, after certain verbs like **credere** (to believe), **pensare** (to think), **dire** (to say), **sperare** (to hope), **finire** (to finish), **smettere** (to stop):

Finisco *di leggere* il giornale e poi esco.	I finish reading the paper and then I go out.
Paolo pensa *di essere* intelligente.	Paolo thinks he is intelligent.
Anna crede *di riuscire* a passare l'esame.	Anna believes she can pass the exam.
La mamma dice *di essere* stanca.	Mum says she's tired.
Devo smettere *di perdere tempo*!	I must stop wasting time!

5 **A** is typically used to express:

place	**Abito *a* Londra.**	I live in London.
	Vado *al* cinema.	I'm going to the cinema.
	Sono *a* casa.	I'm at home.
	La casa si trova *a* 100 metri dal mare.	The house is 100 metres from the sea.
time	**Parto *alle* 17.**	I'm leaving at 17.00.
	Vado in Olanda *a* luglio.	I'm going to Holland in July.

indirect object	**Diamo il libro *a* Silvia.**	We're giving the book to Silvia.
	Scrivete *ai* vostri genitori?	Do you write to your parents?
quality	**Vuoi un gelato *al* limone?**	Do you want a lemon ice-cream?
means/manner	**La giacca è fatta *a* mano.**	The jacket's made by hand.
	Impari tutto *a* memoria?	Do you learn everything by heart?
	Stasera mangiamo patate *al* vapore.	We're having steamed potatoes tonight. [i.e. they're cooked with steam]

A is also used, followed by a verb in the infinitive, after certain verbs like **andare** (to go), **venire** (to come), **cominciare** (to start/begin), **continuare** (to continue), **riuscire** (can/to be able/manage):

'**Dove vai?' 'Vado *a lavorare*.'**	'Where are you going?' 'I'm going to work.'
Vieni *a studiare* in biblioteca?	Are you coming to work in the library?
Comincio *a capire*.	I'm beginning to understand.
Paolo continua *a parlare*.	Paolo continues/keeps on talking.
Non riesco *a sentire* cosa dice.	I can't hear what he's saying.

6 **Da** is typically used to express:

place	**Parto *da* Milano.**	I'm leaving from Milan.
time	**Studio italiano *da* un mese.**	I have been studying Italian for a month.
	aperto *dalle* 9 alle 10	open (from) 9 to 10 (o'clock)
function	**Sono scarpe *da* tennis.**	They're tennis shoes.

Da is always used to mean 'at/at the house of' a person or people:

Abiti *da* tua zia?	Do you live at your aunt's?
Lavoro *da* Anna stasera.	I'm working at Anna's tonight.
Devo andare *dal* dentista.	I have to go to the dentist.

Da is also used followed by an infinitive after **molto** (a lot), **poco** (little), **niente** (nothing), **qualcosa** (something):

Ho molto *da* fare.	I've got a lot to do.
Ha poco *da* dire.	He has little/He's not got much to say.
Non c'è niente *da* bere.	There's nothing to drink.
Vuoi qualcosa *da* mangiare?	Do you want something to eat?

7 **In** is typically used to express:

place	**Vivo *in* campagna.**	I live in the country.
	Abbiamo una casa *in* Francia.	We have a house in France.
time	***nel* 2006**	in 2006
	***nel* ventesimo secolo**	in the twentieth century
means	**Andiamo *in* treno/*in* auto/*in* bici.***	We're going by train/car/on our bikes.

* NB: **in piedi** means 'standing'; 'on foot' is **a piedi**.

8 **Con** is typically used to express:

company	**Vado al cinema *con* Luca.**	I'm going to the cinema with Luca.
	Parlo *con* Anna.	I'm talking to/with Anna.
means	**Devo scrivere *con* una penna rossa.**	I've got to write with a red pen.
	Pago *con* un assegno.	I'm paying with a cheque/by cheque.
manner	**Parla *con* accento straniero.**	He speaks with a foreign accent.
	Parla *con* lentezza.	He speaks slowly.
quality	**una signora *con* i capelli grigi**	a lady with grey hair

9 **Su** is typically used to express:

place	**I tuoi libri sono *sulla* scrivania.**	Your books are on the desk.
	il ponte *sullo* stretto di Messina	the bridge over the Strait of Messina
subject	**un libro *sul* calcio**	a book on/about football

When the preposition **su** is used with a personal pronoun, the pronoun is also preceded by **di**: **Conto *su di* lui** (I'm counting on him).

10 **Per** is typically used to express:

place	**Partiamo *per* la montagna.**	We are leaving for the mountains.
time	**Esco *per* 10 minuti.**	I'm going out for 10 minutes.
	***Per* le 11 sono a casa.**	I'll be home by/for 11.
means	**Mando il file *per* email.**	I'll send the file by email.
cause	**una multa *per* eccesso di velocità**	a fine for speeding/speeding fine
aim	**Studio *per* passare l'esame.**	I'm studying (in order) to pass the exam.
price	***per* 15 euro**	for 15 euros

11 **Tra** and **fra** are typically used to express:

place	*tra* **Milano e Torino**	between Milan and Turin
	fra **compagni di classe**	among classmates
time	*fra* **due ore**	in two hours/two hours' time

Prepositions of place

12 Here are some examples of the different prepositions used to denote place:

Sono *di* **Ferrara.**	I am/come from Ferrara.
La domenica vado *al* **cinema.**	On Sundays I go to the cinema.
Sono *a* **scuola.**	I'm at school.
Vengo *da* **Ferrara.**	I'm coming from Ferrara.
Abito *da* **mia nonna.**	I live at my granny's.
Luisa è *in* **camera sua.**	Luisa is in her room.
Devi camminare *sul* **marciapiedi.**	You have to walk on the pavement.
il ponte *sull'***Arno**	the bridge over the Arno
Partite *per* **Dublino?**	Are you leaving for Dublin?
Novara è *fra* **Torino e Milano.**	Novara is between Turin and Milan.
Siamo *tra* **amici.**	We are among friends.

Another preposition used to denote place is **lungo** (along): **lungo il fiume** (along the river).

13 **A** is normally used with names of town and villages and with cardinal points:

Vado *a* **Pisa.**	I'm going to Pisa.
Abito *a* **Londra.**	I live in London.
Passo le vacanze *a* **Cogne.**	I spend my holidays in Cogne.
Andiamo *a* **nord.**	We are going north.
Cogne è *a* **sud di Aosta.**	Cogne is south of Aosta.

14 **In** is normally used with names of regions and nations, with geographical areas, and with shops:

Vado *in* **Toscana.**	I'm going to Tuscany.
Abito *in* **Inghilterra.**	I live in England.
Passo le vacanze *in* **montagna.***	I spend my holidays in the mountains.
Compro il pane *in* **panetteria.**	I buy bread at the bakery/the baker's.

* With **mare** (sea) the preposition **a** is used (**al mare**, 'at the seaside').

Prepositions of time

15 Some examples of the different prepositions used to denote time:

Di domenica non lavoro.	I don't work on Sundays.
Di sera guardo la tv.	In the evenings I watch TV.
Donatella arriva *alle* 7.	Donatella will arrive at seven.
A Natale rimaniamo a casa.	At Christmas we stay at home.
La scuola finisce *a* giugno.	School ends in June.
nel 2000	in 2000
nel diciottesimo secolo	in the eighteenth century
In autunno piove molto.	In autumn it rains a lot.

16 **Di** is used with the days of the week and parts of the day:

Di lunedì andiamo in piscina.	On Mondays we go to the swimming pool.
Di mattina vado a scuola.	In the morning I go to school.

In these cases, **di** is always used without the definite article.

17 **A** is used with names of festivities, months and hours of the day:

A Pasqua Piera va in Italia.	At Easter Piera is going to Italy.
Il museo riapre *a* marzo.	The museum reopens/will reopen in March.
Il treno parte *alle* 12.	The train is leaving at 12.
Di solito mangiano *a* mezzogiorno.	They normally eat at midday.

18 **In** is used with years, centuries and seasons:

Sono nato *nel* 1990.	I was born in 1990.
Studio il turismo *nel* XIX secolo.	I'm studying tourism in the nineteenth century.
Gli esami sono *in* primavera.	The exams are/will be in the spring.

A or *in*?

19 Sometimes it can be difficult to know whether to use **a** or **in**, so we list below common expressions using these two prepositions:

a casa	(at) home
a scuola	at/to school
a letto	in/to bed
a lezione	in class/to (one's) class
a tavola	to the table [i.e. come and sit down]/at table
a destra/a sinistra	(on/to the) right/left
a nord/a sud/a est/a ovest	(in/to the) north/south/east/west
a colazione/a pranzo/a cena	at/for breakfast/lunch/dinner, supper or tea
a mezzogiorno/a mezzanotte	at midday/midnight
a 10/11/12 [etc.] **anni**	at ten/eleven/twelve [etc.] (years of age)
a metà	in the middle/mid-
all'ombra/al sole	in the shade/in the sun
al bar	in the bar
al ristorante	at/to the restaurant
alla stazione	at/in/to the station
in pizzeria	in/to/at a/the pizzeria/pizza parlour
in discoteca	in/to the disco
in città	in/to town
in centro	in/to the city centre
in chiesa	in/to church
in mensa	in/to the canteen
in camera	in/to the bedroom
in bagno	in/to the bathroom
in classe	in/to the classroom
in palestra	in/to the gym
in caserma	in/to the barracks
in prigione	in/to prison
in ufficio	in/to the office
in piscina	at/to the swimming bath

Compound prepositions

20 Italian also has a number of 'compound prepositions', e.g. **accanto a**, 'next to/beside', **invece di**, 'instead of'. Some of these are always in the compound form, others include **di** only when followed by a personal pronoun. We give here a list of the most common ones:

davanti a	in front of/opposite
vicino a	near/next/close to
fuori da/di	outside
prima di	before
lontano da	far from/a long way from
contro*	against
dentro*	inside
dietro*	behind
dopo*	after
senza*	without
sopra*	on/above
sotto*	under/below
verso*	towards

* When these prepositions are used with a personal pronoun, the pronoun is preceded by the preposition **di** (see Unit 14).

La farmacia è *davanti al* **supermercato.**	The pharmacy is opposite the supermarket.
Abito *lontano dal* **centro.**	I live a long way from the city centre.
L'albergo è *vicino alla* **stazione.**	The hotel is close to the station.
Non esco *senza di* **voi.**	I'm not going out without you.

Exercise 1

Combine the prepositions and the definite articles.

Example: (di) il figlio: del figlio

di	*a*	*da*	*in*	*su*
1 la mamma	8 il mare	15 la zia	22 l'albergo	29 il tavolo
2 lo zio	9 lo stadio	16 lo studente	23 lo stipendio	30 la sedia
3 gli amici	10 la stazione	17 il dentista	24 la casa	31 lo scaffale
4 il parco	11 i ragazzi	18 l'aeroporto	25 gli anni	32 le spalle
5 l'auto	12 gli uomini	19 gli uffici	26 i cassetti	33 i libri
6 i paesi	13 le donne	20 le colleghe	27 le camere	34 gli alberi
7 le stanze	14 l'ospedale	21 i ministri	28 il frigo	35 l'idea

Exercise 2

Complete the sentences with the correct prepositions and, where necessary, combine them with the definite article.

Example: Vengo _____ (la) stazione: <u>dalla</u>

1   Carla abita _____ Budapest.
2   Parigi è _____ Francia.
3   Mangiate _____ (il) ristorante?
4   Torniamo _____ un'ora.
5   Hai molto _____ fare?
6   Devi scrivere _____ (la) nonna.
7   Esco _____ Massimo.
8   Filippo va _____ (il) dentista.
9   Quell'auto è _____ (il) padre di Silvia.
10 Scrivo una lettera _____ (i) miei genitori.
11 Vado _____ Milano _____ treno.
12 Vieni _____ (il) cinema _____ me?
13 Le chiavi sono _____ (il) cassetto.
14 La lezione finisce _____ (le) 11.
15 Studiamo italiano _____ due mesi.
16 Il museo apre _____ (le) 9.00.
17 Compro le rose _____ la zia.
18 Posso parlare _____ Elisa?
19 Vuoi _____ (il) dolce?
20 Il mio compleanno è _____ giugno.

Exercise 3

Complete the sentences with the correct prepositions and, where necessary, combine them with the definite article.

Example: I tuoi libri sono _____ (il) tavolo: <u>sul</u>

1   Domani rimango _____ casa.
2   Sabato andiamo _____ centro.
3   Vado _____ nuotare _____ piscina.
4   Livia è _____ letto: sta poco bene.
5   Puoi comprare una bottiglia _____ aceto?
6   Regalo i CD _____ (il) mio ragazzo.
7   Napoli è _____ sud di Roma.
8   Domani cominciamo _____ lavorare.
9   Parto _____ Roma alle 14 e arrivo _____ Torino alle 21.
10 Ho fame: c'è qualcosa _____ mangiare?
11 Imprestate la bici _____ Maurizio?
12 Vai a scuola _____ autobus?
13 Bardonecchia è _____ montagna.
14 Prendo un gelato _____ (la) fragola.
15 Cosa fate _____ Natale?
16 Piero va _____ (il) supermercato.
17 Il padre _____ (la) mia amica è avvocato.
18 _____ pizzeria c'è sempre molta gente.
19 Paola dorme _____ (la) stanza vicina alla mia.
20 Leggo un libro _____ fantascienza.

Exercise 4

Translate into Italian:

1 I finish working at six.
2 Antonio's leaving for Genoa.
3 Gemma was born in 2001.
4 Fabia never goes out in the evening.
5 Mr and Mrs Bancroft live in the country, in an old villa.
6 The library's behind the gym.
7 You [sing.] can't go out without me!
8 Do you [pl.] live far from the school?
9 Isabella's aunt lives in Greve, in Tuscany.
10 She's got a leather skirt.
11 Angus is from Edinburgh, in Scotland.
12 You have to turn right after the church(, Madam).
13 We're eating at a pizzeria tonight.
14 These flowers are for your [sing.] mother.
15 At Christmas we're going skiing in the mountains.
16 I live near the prison.
17 Margaret's been living in Turin for five years.
18 The train for Aosta leaves from platform 7.
19 We're giving Luisa a CD of Russian music.
20 I always buy the bread at Belli's.

UNIT NINE
Questions

In this unit we will look at the most common ways of asking questions in Italian. We have already seen (Units 4 and 5) that the order of the words in the sentence does not change in the interrogative form; now we need to look at some Italian 'question words'.

1 Chi?

Chi means 'who/whom', or sometimes 'which of', and is only used to refer to people. **Chi** is invariable – that is, the same form is used for masculine and feminine, singular and plural:

Chi è quell'uomo?	Who is that man?
Chi è quella ragazza?	Who is that girl?
Chi sono i tuoi amici?	Who are your friends?
Chi sono quelle ragazze?	Who are those girls?
Chi vuole venire al cinema con me?	Who wants to come to the cinema with me?
Chi viene a cena?	Who's coming for dinner?
Con chi esci?	Who(m) are you going out with?
A chi scrivete?	Who(m) are you writing to?
Chi ha una penna?	Who's got a pen? [i.e. has anyone got a pen?]
Chi non va in gita domani?	Who's not going on the trip tomorrow?
Chi non inviti?	Who(m) aren't you inviting?
Chi di loro parla italiano?	Which of them speaks Italian?

When an adjective refers to **chi**, it must be in the masculine singular form unless it refers to an all-female group:

Chi è pront*o*?	Who is ready?
Chi è soddisfatt*o*?	Who is satisfied?
Chi non è stanc*o*?	Who isn't tired?
Chi di voi (ragazze) è pront*a*?	Which of you (girls) is ready?
Chi di voi (Signori) è italian*o*?	Which of you (gentlemen) is Italian?

2 Che cosa? Cosa? Che?

All three mean 'what' and are used when referring to objects. **Che cosa?**, **Cosa?** and **Che?** are invariable in gender and number:

Cos'è quello?	What's that?
Che cos'è quella luce?	What's that light?
Cosa sono quei segni?	What are those marks?
Che sono quelle costruzioni?	What are those buildings?
Che succede?	What's happening?
Che cosa volete?	What do you want?
Cosa studi?	What are you studying/do you study?
Cosa posso fare per Lei?	What can I do for you?
A che pensate?	What are you thinking about?

Che is also used as an adjective meaning 'what (sort/type of)':

Che lavoro fai?	What's your job? [lit. what work do you do?]
Che musica ascolti di solito?	What (sort of) music do you usually listen to?
Che film vai a vedere?	What film are you going to see?
Che auto compra tuo padre?	What (make of) car is your father going to buy?

3 Come?

Come means 'how':

Come sta, Signora?	How are you, Madam?
Come va?	How's it going?
Come fate la pizza?	How do you make (a) pizza?

Come can sometimes mean 'what', as in **Come dici?** (What did you say?), **Com'è Edimburgo/il nuovo professore?** (What's Edinburgh/the new teacher like?).

4 Dove?

Dove means 'where':

Dove abiti?	Where do you live?
Dove andate?	Where are you going?
Dove sono le chiavi?	Where are the keys?
Dov'è il mio libro?	Where is my book?

5 Quando?

Quando means 'when':

Quando partono i tuoi amici?	When are your friends leaving?
Quando comincia il film?	When does the film start?
Quando arriva il treno?	When does the train arrive?
Quando è lo sciopero dei treni?	When's the rail/train strike?

6 Perché?

Perché means 'why':

Perché ridono?	Why are they laughing?
Perché Giulia non va a scuola?	Why isn't Giulia going to school?
Perché non studi?	Why don't you study?

Come mai has a similar meaning, corresponding to the English 'how come':

Come mai non mangi?	How come you're not eating?
Come mai siete in ritardo?	How come you are late?

7 Quanto?

Quanto means 'how much' when referring to quantity, and 'how long', 'how far', 'how tall', etc. when it refers to time, distance, height, etc.:

Quanto pesa?	How much/What does it weigh?
Quanto costa questa maglietta?	How much/What does this T-shirt cost?
Quanto dura il film?	How long does the film last?
Quanto è alta tua sorella?	How tall is your sister?
Quant'è?	How much is it?

Quanto can also be used as an adjective or pronoun. In such cases it agrees in gender and number with the noun it refers to: **quanto** [ms], **quanta** [fs] (how much), **quanti** [mp], **quante** [fp] (how many):

Quanto pane devo comprare?	How much bread do I have to buy?
Quanta pasta vuoi?	How much pasta do you want?
Quanti esercizi dobbiamo fare?	How many exercises have we got to do?
Quante ragazze ci sono in classe tua?	How many girls are there in your class?
Quanto tempo abbiamo?	How much time is there?/How long have we got?
'Ci sono molte persone.' '**Quante?**'	'There are a lot of people.' 'How many?'
'**Dobbiamo comprare del pane.**' '**Quanto?**'	'We must get (some) bread.' 'How much?'

8 Quale?

Quale means 'which' (or sometimes 'what'). It is used either as an adjective or as a pronoun, and therefore agrees with the noun it refers to: **quale**, 'which (one)', **quali**, 'which (ones)'. The use of **quale** rather than **che** usually implies that there is a choice, as for example if there are some books lying on the table: **Quale libro leggi?** 'Which book are you reading?':

Quale canzone preferisci?	Which song do you prefer?
Quali esercizi facciamo?	Which exercises are we doing?
Quali sono i tuoi libri?	Which are your books?
'Compro due giornali.' 'Quali?'	'I'm buying two papers.' 'Which ones?'
Qual è la canzone più famosa?*	Which/What is the best-known song?
Qual è il Suo indirizzo/numero di telefono?*	What's your address/phone number?

* **Qual** (without an apostrophe) is used before the forms of **essere** starting with a vowel; used in this way, it sometimes means 'what' rather than 'which'.

9 As is seen in some of the examples in paragraphs 2, 3, 4 and 7, **cosa**, **che cosa**, **come**, **dove** and **quanto** can also be shortened before the forms of **essere** starting with a vowel, becoming **cos'**, **che cos'**, **com'**, **dov'** and **quant'** (all *with* an apostrophe):

Cos'era quel rumore?	What was that noise?
Che cos'è successo?	What happened?
Com'era lo spettacolo?	How was the show?
Dov'è la stazione?	Where is the station?
Quant'è costato?	How much did it cost?

Exercise 1

Complete the sentences with **chi** or **che/cosa/che cosa** as appropriate.

Examples: _____ mi cerca?: chi; _____ fate?: che/cosa/che cosa

1 _____ sono quei signori?
2 _____ di loro è tuo cugino?
3 Con _____ uscite stasera?
4 _____ posso fare per te?
5 _____ studiate?
6 _____ viene con me?
7 _____ accompagna Luca?
8 _____ vuoi bere?
9 Di _____ è questo libro?
10 _____ succede?

11 Per _____ lavori?
12 _____ preferisci? Caffè o te?
13 A _____ telefoni?
14 _____ viene alla festa?
15 _____ dici?
16 _____ preferisci? Gianni o Piero?
17 _____ leggi?
18 Da _____ vai a cena?
19 _____ vuoi fare stasera?
20 _____ apre la porta?

Exercise 2

Complete the questions with an appropriate word (**che, come, dove, quando, perché** or **quale/quali/qual**).

Examples: '_____ non esci stasera?' 'Devo studiare.': perché; '_____ è la tua bici?' 'Quella.': qual

1 '_____ abitate?' 'A Milano.'
2 '_____ parte l'autobus?' 'Alle 8.00.'
3 '_____ non studi?' 'Non sto bene.'
4 '_____ sta, Professore?' 'Bene, grazie.'
5 '_____ è il tuo compleanno?' 'Il 20 aprile.'
6 '_____ lavoro fa tuo padre?' 'Il medico.'
7 '_____ strada devo prendere?' 'Quella a destra.'
8 '_____ è la mensa?' 'Dietro la palestra.'
9 '_____ sei in ritardo?' 'C'è sciopero degli autobus.'
10 '_____ è il tuo indirizzo?' 'Via Garibaldi 22.'

11 '_____ genere di musica ascoltate?' 'Rock.'
12 '_____ materia preferisci?' 'Scienze.'
13 '_____ ti vesti per la festa?' 'Con la gonna lunga.'
14 '_____ metto la bici?' 'In garage.'
15 '_____ non venite con noi?' 'Abbiamo sonno.'
16 '_____ è il parcheggio?' 'Davanti al cinema.'
17 '_____ comincia la scuola?' 'A settembre.'
18 '_____ è la capitale dell'Italia?' 'Roma.'
19 '_____ non vai in vacanza?' 'Non ho soldi.'
20 '_____ libri leggi?' 'Romanzi di avventure.'

Exercise 3

Complete the sentences with the correct form of **quanto**.

Examples: _____ anni hai?: <u>quanti</u>; _____ costa questa maglietta?: <u>quanto</u>

1 _____ persone vengono?
2 Fra _____ tempo partite?
3 _____ fratelli ha Luisa?
4 _____ esercizi fate?
5 _____ stanze ha la tua casa?
6 _____ gente inviti?
7 _____ sei alto?
8 _____ pagine dobbiamo studiare?
9 _____ mesi rimanete in Italia?
10 _____ guadagni?
11 _____ frutta devo comprare?
12 _____ costano quei jeans?
13 _____ autobus devi prendere?
14 _____ dura il concerto?
15 Da _____ studiate italiano?
16 _____ cartoline spedisci?
17 _____ spendi al mese?
18 _____ amiche hai?
19 _____ libri devi leggere?
20 _____ è lontana la discoteca?

Exercise 4

1 How many rolls do you [pl.] want?
2 Where are you [pl.] going for lunch?
3 Who are those people?
4 What are you [sing.] doing on Sunday?
5 When are you [pl.] going on holiday?
6 Why isn't Luisa leaving?
7 Which is your [sing.] bike?
8 What film are you [sing.] watching?
9 Which of them is Italian?
10 When does the train arrive?

UNIT TEN
Indirect object pronouns (1)

1 We saw in Unit 7 that a direct object is the person or thing that the verb directly impacts on. An *indirect* object is the person or thing that the action is happening *to* or *for*: **Scrivo *a Carla* domani** (I'll write *to Carla* tomorrow); **Mando cartoline *a tutti i miei amici*** (I send cards *to all my friends*). In English, the indirect object can usually be preceded by 'to' or 'for', but these are very often omitted: compare 'I gave the book *to Karen*' and 'I gave *Karen* the book', or 'I'll pour a glass *for Jane*' and 'I'll pour *Jane* a glass'.

An indirect object pronoun replaces a noun used as an indirect object: 'I gave the book *to her*/I gave *her* the book', 'I'll pour *her* a glass/I'll pour a glass for *her*'.

In Italian, an indirect object pronoun replaces a noun preceded by the preposition **a**; it has to agree in gender and number with the noun it refers to. Indirect object pronouns normally come before the verb. In the following examples, the pronouns are in italics:

Quando vedo Maria *le* racconto tutto.   When I see Maria I'll tell *her*
   [**le** stands for **a Maria** (fs)]   everything.
Non telefono a Carlo, *gli* scrivo.   I'm not going to phone Carlo: I'll
   [**gli** stands for **a Carlo** (ms)]   write to *him*.
Paolo non *ci* dice mai la verità.   Paolo never tells *us* the truth.
   [**ci** stands for **a noi**]

2 The forms of the indirect object pronouns are as follows:

mi	to me
ti	to you
gli [m]/**le** [f]	to him/it/her
ci	to us
vi	to you
gli [m and f]	to them

The third person plural pronoun **gli** is used for both masculine and feminine. For the third person plural, **loro** can be used instead of **gli**, but it always follows the verb; the meaning is the same, but the use of **loro** is far less frequent and is more formal.

Mi **mandi una cartolina da Roma?**	Will you send *me* a postcard from Rome?
Vi **scrivo appena arrivo.**	I'll write to *you* as soon as I arrive.
È il compleanno di Anna: *le* **regalo un CD.**	It's Anna's birthday: I'm giving *her* a CD.
Se Dario non ha l'auto, *gli* **dò un passaggio.**	If Dario hasn't got his car, I'll give *him* a lift.
Ti **impresto i soldi.**	I'll lend *you* the money.
'Scrivi agli zii?' 'No, *gli* **telefono domani/No, telefono** *loro* **domani.'**	'Are you going to write to your uncles?' 'No, I'll phone *them* tomorrow.'
Gli **dico la verità/Dico** *loro* **la verità.**	I'm going to tell *them* the truth.

Negative form

3 The negative is formed by putting **non** before the pronoun:

Non *ti* **impresto i soldi.**	I won't lend *you* the money.
Non *le* **scrivo,** *le* **telefono.**	I'm not going to write (to *her*), I'll phone *her*.
Non *gli* **rispondo.**	I'm not going to reply to/answer *him*.

4 When an indirect object pronoun is used with a verb in the infinitive (usually after verbs like **dovere**, **potere**, **volere** or **sapere**), it can be attached to the infinitive, which drops the final vowel:

Le **voglio parlare.**	*or*	**Voglio parlar***le***.**	I want to talk to *her*.
Gli **devo scrivere.**	*or*	**Devo scriver***gli***.**	I must write to *him*/them.
Mi **potete telefonare?**	*or*	**Potete telefonar***mi***?**	Can you phone *me*?
Mi **sai dire quando?**	*or*	**Sai dir***mi* **quando?**	Can you tell *me* when?

Each pair of sentences has exactly the same meaning – the form used makes no difference.

Formal form

5 The indirect object pronouns used for the formal form are **Le** for the singular (for both women and men) and **Vi** for the plural (the pronoun **Loro** – after the verb – can also be used, but this is very formal):

Le **rispondo subito, Signor Colli.**	I'll answer *you* immediately, Mr Colli.
Le **dò un passaggio, Signora Banfi.**	I'll give *you* a lift, Mrs Banfi.
Signori Bianco, *Vi* telefono domani.	(Mr and Mrs Bianco,) I'll phone *you* tomorrow.
(Signori Bianco, telefono *Loro* domani.)	

Exercise 1

Rewrite the sentences, replacing the words in italics with the correct indirect object pronoun.

Example: Scrivete *a Luigi?*: Gli scrivete?

1 Telefoniamo *a Carla*.
2 Spedisco le cartoline *ai miei amici*.
3 Silvia racconta una storia *al bambino*.
4 Regalo un libro *alla zia*.
5 Anna scrive *alle amiche*.
6 Porto i fiori *alla nonna*.
7 Scriviamo *ai nostri compagni*.
8 Olga e Silvia parlano *a Giulia*.
9 La nonna legge un libro *ai nipoti*.
10 Cosa regalate *a Marco*?

Exercise 2

Change the sentences into the negative.

Example: Gli scrivo: Non gli scrivo.

1 Le parlo di lavoro.
2 Mi telefoni?
3 Vi regalo dei libri.
4 Gli offrite qualcosa?
5 Gli amici le offrono un gelato.
6 Ci scrivete?
7 Ti mando una cartolina.
8 Vi restituisco il libro.
9 Paolo mi dice la verità.
10 Gli spedisco il pacco.

Exercise 3

Rewrite the sentences, changing the position of the pronoun.

Example: Li devi comprare: Devi comprarli.

1 Le possiamo scrivere?
2 Ti devo parlare.
3 Gli voglio regalare una chitarra.
4 Ci puoi telefonare?
5 Vi devono offrire qualcosa!

6 Mi potete dire tutto.
7 Le posso parlare, Signora?
8 Non gli dovete scrivere.
9 Non ti posso rispondere.
10 Le voglio credere.

Exercise 4

Complete the sentences with the appropriate indirect object pronouns.

Examples: Mauro ha molti amici e _____ telefona spesso: gli; Livia vuole
parlare con te, devi telefonar_____ : le

1 'Telefonate a Luisa?' 'No, _____ scriviamo una lettera.'
2 Se mi chiedi qualcosa, _____ rispondo.
3 'Cosa regali a tuo padre?' '_____ regalo una cravatta.'
4 Se vedi le mie amiche, puoi dir_____ che le aspetto per domani?
5 Signora, posso offrir_____ un caffè?
6 'Ci portate un regalo, dall'Italia?' 'Sì, _____ portiamo un panettone.'
7 'Cosa vuoi dir_____?' 'Vi voglio dire la verità.'
8 Gianni, _____ presento mia sorella.
9 'Quando telefoni ai nonni?' '_____ telefono domani sera.'
10 Professore, _____ devo parlare.
11 Non so fare questo esercizio: _____ dai una mano?
12 Domani è il compleanno di Anna: devo far_____ gli auguri.
13 Paolo dice sempre bugie: non _____ dovete credere.
14 Telefono a Michele e _____ chiedo un prestito.
15 Se non avete l'auto, _____ dò un passaggio.
16 Se Carla e Pietro hanno bisogno di soldi, _____ posso fare un prestito.
17 'Quanto ti danno all'ora?' '_____ danno 15 euro.'
18 Appena vedo Silvia _____ rendo i libri.
19 Se vuoi, _____ impresto la mia bici.
20 Ettore è un buon amico e _____ racconto sempre tutto.

Exercise 5

Translate into Italian:

1 Can you [sing.] tell Lucia that I want to speak to her?
2 As soon as I arrive in Rome I'll phone you [pl.].
3 I have to ask you a favour, Madam.
4 Are you [sing.] giving them your phone number?
5 They always tell us interesting things.
6 They always send me a card when they go to Italy.
7 For her birthday, I'm giving her flowers.
8 I've got to give you [sing.] Luca's books.
9 If you [pl.] want, I'll tell you a story.
10 Massimo writes to me every week.

UNIT ELEVEN
Piacere and similar verbs

1 **Piacere** corresponds to 'to like', but it is used in a different way from its English counterpart. In Italian, the subject of the verb/sentence is the thing or person one likes; the person who likes something is denoted by an indirect object pronoun (see Unit 10):

Mi piace lo sport.	I like sport. [lit. sport is pleasing to me]
Ti piace ballare?	Do you like dancing? [lit. is dancing pleasing to you?]
Mi piacciono i gatti.	I like cats. [lit. cats are pleasing to me]

2 **Piacere** is an irregular verb mostly used in the third person singular (**piace**) and plural (**piacciono**). As can be seen in the examples, **piace** is used if the thing that one likes is a singular noun or pronoun, or the infinitive of a verb; **piacciono** is used if the things that one likes are a plural noun or pronoun:

Singular noun or pronoun

mi (to me)	piace	**la mia città.**	I like my home town.
ti (to you)	piace	**questo/questa.**	You like this (one).
gli/le (to him/her)	piace	**il calcio.**	He/she likes football.
ci (to us)	piace	**la musica rock.**	We like rock music.
vi (to you)	piace	**il tennis.**	You like tennis.
gli (to them)	piace	**quello/quella.**	They like that one.

Verb

mi (to me)	piace	**leggere.**	I like to read/reading.
ti (to you)	piace	**andare in bici.**	You like to cycle/cycling.
gli/le (to him/her)	piace	**sciare.**	He/she likes to ski/skiing.
ci (to us)	piace	**guardare la tv.**	We like to watch/watching TV.
vi (to you)	piace	**dormire.**	You like to sleep/sleeping.
gli (to them)	piace	**ballare.**	They like to dance/dancing.

Plural noun or pronoun

mi (to me)	**piacciono**	**questi/queste.**	I like these.
ti (to you)	**piacciono**	**le ciliegie.**	You like cherries.
gli/le (to him/her)	**piacciono**	**i romanzi.**	He/she likes novels.
ci (to us)	**piacciono**	**quelli/quelle.**	We like those.
vi (to you)	**piacciono**	**gli scherzi.**	You like practical jokes.
gli (to them)	**piacciono**	**le auto veloci.**	They like fast cars.

3 The negative is formed by putting **non** before the pronoun:

Non mi piace la pizza.	I don't like pizza.
Non ti piace questo/questa?	Don't you like this (one)?
Non le piace sciare.	She doesn't like skiing.
Non ci piacciono i videogiochi.	We don't like video games.

4 As usual, for the polite form in the singular the feminine pronoun (**Le**) is used for both men and women; for the plural **Vi** is normally used:

Le piacciono i funghi, Signora Vanni?	Do you like mushrooms, Mrs Vanni?
Le piace leggere, Signor Vanni?	Do you like reading, Mr Vanni?
Non Le piace quello/quella?	Don't you like that one?
Non Le piace sciare?	Don't you like skiing?
Signori Conti, Vi piace l'Italia?	Do you like Italy, Mr and Mrs Conti?
Signori Conti, piace Loro l'Italia?*	Do you like Italy, Mr and Mrs Conti?

* **Loro** is a much more formal way of addressing people in the plural; it is always placed after the verb.

5 When the person who likes something is denoted not by a pronoun but by a noun, the noun must be preceded by the preposition **a**:

A **Claudia non piace andare a scuola.**	Claudia doesn't like going to school.
Allo **zio Davide piace la musica classica.**	Uncle Davide likes classical music.
A **Piera non piacciono questi/queste.**	Piera doesn't like these.
Ai **miei nonni piace dormire.**	My grandparents like sleeping.
A **Franco e Luisa piace viaggiare.**	Franco and Luisa like travelling.

6 To mark a contrast, the stressed forms of the pronouns (**a me**, **a te**, **a lui/a lei**, **a noi**, **a voi**, **a loro** – see Unit 14) are used instead of the unstressed forms:

A me piace il caffè, *a te* piace il te.	I like coffee, you like tea.
A lui piacciono i gatti, *a lei* no.	He likes cats, she doesn't.
A noi piace il calcio, *a voi* il tennis.	We like football, you like tennis.
A loro piace nuotare, *a noi* piace sciare.	They like swimming, we like skiing.
A me piace questo/questa, *a Lei* quello/ quella.	I like this one, you like that one.

7 There are other verbs which are used in the same way as **piacere**: **mancare** (to miss) [lit. 'to be lacking/missing']; **servire** (to need) [lit. 'to be useful']; **bastare** (to be enough/sufficient) and **sembrare** and **parere** (to seem):

Mi manca il mio ragazzo.	I miss my boyfriend. [lit. my boyfriend is lacking to me]
Non vi mancano i vostri genitori?	Don't you miss your parents? [lit. aren't your parents lacking to you?]
Ti serve una penna?	Do you need a pen?
A Livia servono i tuoi consigli.	Livia needs your advice.
Questi/queste non ci bastano.	These aren't enough for us.
A me bastano 10 euro e a te?	10 euros are sufficient for me – are they for you/how about you?
Il comportamento di Carlo mi sembra/mi pare strano.	Carlo's behaviour seems strange to me.
Non mi sembra/mi pare giusto.	It doesn't seem fair to me/I don't think it's fair.

Exercise 1

Rewrite the sentences, replacing the words in italics with the correct pronoun.

Example: *A Sara* non piace il caffè: Non le piace il caffè.

1   *A Federica* non piacciono i carciofi.
2   *A Giampiero* non piace guidare.
3   *A Massimo* piace viaggiare.
4   *A Tullio e Anna* piace il mare.
5   *Ai miei amici* piace ballare.
6   *A me e a Marco* non piace il pesce.
7   *A te e a Marina* piace nuotare?
8   *A Mara* piacciono i film francesi.
9   *Alla mamma* non piace stirare.
10   *Allo zio* piace andare in moto.

Exercise 2

Change the sentences into the negative.

Example: Mi piace la pioggia: Non mi piace la pioggia.

1 Le piace andare in centro il sabato.
2 Ti piace la musica classica?
3 Gli piacciono i funghi.
4 Vi piace guardare la televisione?
5 Mi piacciono i film di fantascienza.
6 Gli piace la scuola.
7 Ci piacciono le canzoni italiane.
8 Le piacciono gli spaghetti.
9 Mi piace sciare.
10 Vi piace la cioccolata al latte?

Exercise 3

Write sentences expressing your taste.

Example: cavalli: (Non) mi piacciono i cavalli.

1 la frutta; 2 il calcio; 3 le fragole; 4 giocare a tennis; 5 uscire con gli amici;
6 i gatti; 7 la pizza; 8 i dolci; 9 ballare; 10 le vacanze

Exercise 4

Taking the words in the two columns below, write affirmative or negative
sentences using the verb **piacere**.

Example: Maria   le patate: A Maria (non) piacciono le patate.

1 Luigi   il caffè senza zucchero
2 il professore   le poesie di Leopardi
3 mia sorella   andare al cinema
4 i miei cugini   i film di Fellini
5 il primo ministro   la politica

Exercise 5

Supply the correct form of the verbs in brackets.

Example: Quei libri mi (sembrare) interessanti: sembrano

1 Ci (bastare) questo pane?
2 Vi (sembrare) bello quel film?
3 Ci (piacere) le auto sportive.
4 A Sebastiano (mancare) la mamma!
5 'Voglio comprare una moto.' 'Ti (servire) dei soldi?'
6 A Livio (mancare) i soldi per le vacanze.

7 Quello che dici mi (sembrare) interessante.
8 Mi (servire) delle scarpe nuove.
9 Quale di quei due libri ti (parere) migliore?
10 Non ti (bastare) 20 euro?

Exercise 6

Translate into Italian, using the verbs **piacere**, **sembrare**, **servire**, **mancare** or
bastare.

1 An hour isn't enough for me!
2 Giovanni needs a pen.
3 Lynne's missing her Italian friends.
4 Do you [sing.] like chocolate?
5 She doesn't like going to the cinema.
6 Do you [pl.] need a lift?
7 They need a pen and a notebook.
8 Do you find the show boring, Madam?
9 Do you [sing.] need help?
10 I like reading.

UNIT TWELVE
The present perfect tense

Use of the present perfect

1 The present perfect ('passato prossimo') is one of the two most used past tenses of the indicative in Italian (the other is the imperfect ('imperfetto')). The present perfect is often used like the English present perfect (e.g. 'I *have seen* it', 'She *has gone* home') to state that an action has happened in the past, but that its effects are still lasting in the present. However, in Northern Italy and in the language of the media, it is also equivalent to the English simple past (e.g. 'I *saw* it', 'She *went* home'), referring to actions which happened in a more distant past and have no immediate consequences in the present. Indeed, it more often corresponds to the English simple past than to the English present perfect. In other words, in Italian, the difference between present perfect ('passato prossimo') and simple past ('passato remoto') is not always marked, and it is always possible to use the former:

Napoleone è morto il 5 maggio 1821.	Napoleon died on 5 May 1821.
L'estate scorsa siamo andati in vacanza sul lago di Garda.	Last summer we went to Lake Garda for our/a holiday.
Nina è nata in Russia.	Nina was born in Russia.
L'anno scorso, mi hanno regalato una mountain bike.	Last year, they gave me a mountain bike.

2 The present perfect is a compound tense and is formed, as in English, with the present tense of the auxiliary verb followed by the past participle of the verb:

Ho visto **un bel film.**	I saw/*have seen* a lovely film.
Ha telefonato **Marco.**	Marco phoned/*has phoned*.
Sono rimasto **a casa.**	I stayed/*have stayed* at home.
Anna *è uscita.*	Anna went out/*has gone* out.
Sono andati **in piscina?**	Did they go/*Have* they *gone* to the swimming pool?

As the examples confirm, the 'passato prossimo' may correspond to either the simple past or the present perfect in English. But there are also other differences between the Italian and English structures: there is only one auxiliary verb in English ('to have'), but in Italian there is a choice of two, **avere** and **essere**; when **essere** is used, the past participle has to agree in gender and number with the subject; finally, whether to use **avere** or **essere** is not usually a *free* choice. We will look at all these differences in detail, but first we need to look at the forms of the Italian past participle.

Forms of the past participle

3 The regular forms of the past participle are obtained by changing the ending of the infinitive as follows:

Infinitive in -are	*Infinitive in -ere*	*Infinitive in -ire*
-ato	**-uto**	**-ito**

Infinitive	*Past participle*	
parlare	**parlato**	(to speak) spoken
mangiare	**mangiato**	(to eat) eaten
cadere	**caduto**	(to fall) fallen
volere	**voluto**	(to want) wanted
piacere	**piaciuto***	(to like) liked
conoscere	**conosciuto***	(to know/meet for the first time) known/met
partire	**partito**	(to leave) left
capire	**capito**	(to understand) understood

* Verbs ending in **-cere** (or **-scere**) keep the 'soft' sound of **c** (or **sc**) and therefore add an **i** before the **-uto** ending (**-iuto**).

The past participle of verbs in **-urre** ends in **-otto**:

Infinitive	*Past participle*	
condurre	**condotto**	(to lead/drive/manage) led/driven/managed
tradurre	**tradotto**	(to translate) translated
produrre	**prodotto**	(to produce) produced

4 In Italian, as in most languages, many verbs have an irregular past participle, which is best learned by heart and with use. Here is a list of the most frequently used:

Infinitive	Past participle	
accendere	acceso	(to turn on/switch on) turned on/switched on
aprire	aperto	(to open) opened
bere	bevuto	(to drink) drunk
chiedere	chiesto	(to ask) asked
chiudere	chiuso	(to close) closed
decidere	deciso	(to decide) decided
dire	detto	(to say/tell) said/told
essere	stato*	(to be) been
fare	fatto	(to do/make) done/made
leggere	letto	(to read) read
mettere	messo	(to put/put on) put/put on
perdere	perso/perduto**	(to lose) lost
prendere	preso	(to take) taken
rendere	reso	(to return/give back) returned/given back
rimanere	rimasto	(to remain/stay) remained/stayed
rispondere	risposto	(to answer) answered
rompere	rotto	(to break) broken
scendere	sceso	(to go down/descend) gone down/descended
scrivere	scritto	(to write) written
spegnere	spento	(to turn off/switch off) turned off/switched off
spendere	speso	(to spend) spent
succedere	successo	(to happen) happened
togliere	tolto	(to take away/off) taken away/off
vedere	visto/veduto**	(to see) seen
venire	venuto	(to come) come
vincere	vinto	(to win) won
vivere	vissuto	(to live) lived

* **Stato** is also the past participle of **stare**.
** The regular forms **perduto** and **veduto** are rarely used.

The present perfect

5 The present perfect in Italian is formed with the present indicative of **avere** or **essere** (auxiliary verbs) followed by the past participle of the verb. Here are two examples, one using **avere** and the other **essere**:

Present of avere	Past participle of scrivere	
(io) **ho**	**scritto**	I wrote/have written
(tu) **hai**	**scritto**	you wrote/have written
(lui/lei) **ha**	**scritto**	he/she/it wrote/has written
(noi) **abbiamo**	**scritto**	we wrote/have written
(voi) **avete**	**scritto**	you wrote/have written
(loro) **hanno**	**scritto**	they wrote/have written

Present of essere	Past participle of andare	
(io) **sono**	**andato/andata**	I went/have gone
(tu) **sei**	**andato/andata**	you went/have gone
(lui/lei) **è**	**andato/andata**	he/she/it went/has gone
(noi) **siamo**	**andati/andate**	we went/have gone
(voi) **siete**	**andati/andate**	you went/have gone
(loro) **sono**	**andati/andate**	they went/have gone

6 As can be seen, when the present perfect is formed with **avere** the past participle does not change; but when the present perfect is formed with **essere** the past participle behaves like an adjective, agreeing in gender and number with the subject of the verb. Here are some examples:

Avere

Livia ha guardato la televisione.	Livia (has) watched TV.
Hai comprato il pane?	Did you buy/Have you bought the bread?
Ha prenotato, Signor Ferro?	Did you book/Have you booked, Mr Ferro?

Essere

Monica è uscita. [fs]	Monica went out/Monica's gone out.
Pietro è stato malato. [ms]	Pietro's been ill.
Fabia e Silvia sono rimaste a casa. [fp]	Fabia and Silvia (have) stayed at home.
Giulia e Sebastiano sono partiti. [mp]	Giulia and Sebastiano (have) left.
Sono andata al cinema. [fs]	I went/I've been to the cinema. [the speaker is female]
Siamo arrivati tardi. [mp]	We (have) arrived late. [the speakers are males or a mixed group]
Signor Poli, Lei quando è arrivato?* [ms]	When did you arrive, Mr Poli?
Signora Poli, Lei quando è arrivata?* [fs]	When did you arrive, Mrs Poli?

* When the polite form is used and the auxiliary is **essere**, the past participle agrees with the gender of the person being spoken to, not with **Lei**.

Present perfect of *avere* and *essere*

7 **Avere** forms the present perfect with the auxiliary **avere**:

ho avuto	I had/have had
hai avuto	you had/have had
ha avuto	he/she/it had/has had
abbiamo avuto	we had/have had
avete avuto	you had/have had
hanno avuto	they had/have had

Essere forms the present perfect with the auxiliary **essere**:

sono stato/stata	I was/have been
sei stato/stata	you were/have been
è stato/stata	he/she/it was/has been
siamo stati/state	we were/have been
siete stati/state	you were/have been
sono stati/state	they were/have been

La settimana scorsa abbiamo avuto ospiti.	Last week we had guests.
Tanya ha avuto la varicella.	Tanya has had chickenpox.
Nina è stata malata.	Nina has been ill.
Des è stato mio studente.	Des was a student of mine.

8 Like the present, the present perfect of **essere** can be used with the pronoun **ci** (see Unit 4): **c'è stato/stata** (there was/has been), **ci sono stati/state** (there were/have been):

C'è stata un'alluvione.	There was/has been a flood.
Ci sono stati troppo incidenti.	There were/have been too many accidents.

Essere or *avere*?

9 Deciding whether to use **essere** or **avere** can be a bit of a problem. The only firm rules are those governing *transitive* verbs (i.e. verbs which can have a direct object) and *reflexive* verbs (see Unit 20). Transitive verbs always use **avere**; reflexive verbs always use **essere**.

As for intransitive verbs, some use **avere** and others **essere**. In general, it can be said that verbs of movement (such as **andare** (to go), **venire** (to come), **partire** (to leave), **uscire** (to go out), **entrare** (to go in/come in)) or non-movement (such as **rimanere** (to remain), **restare** (to stay/remain)), and verbs of state (such as **essere**, **diventare** (to become), **cambiare** (to change), **crescere** (to grow)) use the auxiliary **essere**. However, this is not a hard and fast rule: there are intransitive verbs which take **avere**.

Ho conosciuto i genitori di Gianni. [transitive]	I (have) met Gianni's parents.
Avete spedito le vostre cartoline? [transitive]	Did you send/Have you sent your postcards?
Quanto hai speso? [transitive]	How much did you spend?
Ieri sera siamo andati a un concerto rock. [intransitive]	Last night we went to a rock concert.
Domenica scorsa siamo rimasti a casa. [intransitive]	Last Sunday we stayed at home.
Il tempo è cambiato. [intransitive]	The weather's changed.
Ho dormito bene. [intransitive]	I slept well.

To help in choosing the right auxiliary, here is a list of common verbs which form the present perfect with **essere**:

Infinitive	*Present perfect*	
andare	sono andato/-a	I went/have gone
arrivare	sono arrivato/-a	I arrived/have arrived
bastare*	è bastato/-a	it was/has been enough
	sono bastati/-e	they were/have been enough
costare*	è costato/-a	it cost/has cost
	sono costati/-e	they cost/have cost
crescere	sono cresciuto/-a	I grew/have grown
diventare	sono diventato/-a	I became/have become
entrare	sono entrato/-a	I went/have gone in/I entered/have entered
essere	sono stato/-a	I was/have been
morire*	è morto/-a	he/she/it died/has died
	sono morti/-e	
nascere	sono nato/-a	I was born
partire	sono partito/-a	I left/have left
piacere*	è piaciuto/-a	it pleased/has pleased
	sono piaciuti/-e	they pleased/have pleased
restare	sono restato/-a	I stayed/remained/I have stayed/remained
rimanere	sono rimasto/-a	I stayed/remained/I have stayed/remained
(ri)tornare	sono (ri)tornato/-a	I came back/have come back
riuscire	sono riuscito/-a	I succeeded/managed/I have succeeded/managed
sembrare	sono sembrato/-a	I seemed/have seemed
stare	sono stato/-a	I stood/stayed/I have stood/stayed
succedere*	è successo/-a	it happened/has happened
	sono successi/-e	they happened/have happened
uscire	sono uscito/-a	I went out/have gone out
venire	sono venuto/-a	I came/have come

* These verbs are normally only used in the third person singular and plural:

I soldi sono bastati.	The money was enough.
Quanto è costata quella bici?	How much did that bicycle cost?
La bici è costata più di 900 euro.	The bike cost over 900 euros.
Molti civili sono morti.	Many civilians died/have died.
Le è piaciuto il film, Signora?	Did you like the film(, Madam)?
Da allora sono succese molte cose.*	Since then many things have happened/ After that many things happened.

* Note that **succedere** is an impersonal verb: something or things can happen, but **succedere** cannot be used like the English '*I happened to be* in Rome' etc.

Negative form

10   The negative is formed by putting **non** before the auxiliary:

Ieri non sono andato a scuola.	I didn't go to school yesterday.
Lisa non è riuscita a finire quel lavoro.	Lisa didn't manage/hasn't managed to finish that job.
Non hai telefonato a Fabia?	Didn't you phone/Haven't you phoned Fabia?

11   The adverbs **ancora** (again), **mai** (ever), **più** (more/again) and **già** (already) are normally placed between the auxiliary and the verb (e.g. **Ho *già* risposto** (I've already replied)). When they are used in the negative – **non . . . ancora** (not . . . yet), **non . . . mai** (never), **non . . . più** (not . . . any more/not . . . again/ no . . . longer) (see also Unit 6, paragraph 2) – **non** is placed before the auxiliary:

Sei *ancora* andato in biblioteca?	Did you go/Have you been to the library again?
Siete *mai* stati su un ghiacciaio?	Have you ever been on a glacier?
Hai *più* visto i tuoi amici?	Have you (ever) seen your friends again?
***Non* abbiamo *ancora* preso il biglietto.**	We haven't bought the ticket yet.
Paola *non* è *mai* stata a Venezia.	Paola has never been to Venice.
Carlo *non* ha *più* telefonato.	Carlo didn't phone/hasn't (ever) phoned again.

Dovere, potere, volere

12 The present perfect of **dovere**, **potere** and **volere** is normally formed with the auxiliary **avere**, but when they are followed by a verb which forms the present perfect with **essere**, they may take **essere** as well; if **essere** is used, the past participle of the verb agrees with the subject:

I nostri amici hanno dovuto partire.	Our friends had to leave.
I nostri amici sono dovut*i* partire.	
Cecilia non ha potuto andare in Irlanda.	Cecilia couldn't go to Ireland.
Cecilia non è potut*a* andare in Irlanda.	
Perché non avete voluto uscire?	Why didn't you want to go out?
Perché non siete volut*i* uscire?	

Remember that it is never wrong to use **avere**:

Ho dovuto lavorare.	I (have) had to work.
Maria ha dovuto rimanere a casa.	Maria (has) had to stay at home.
Elena non ha potuto telefonare.	Elena couldn't/hasn't been able to phone.
Elena e Sergio non hanno potuto entrare.	Elena and Sergio couldn't/haven't been able to get in.

Exercise 1

Supply the correct endings for the past participles, ensuring that they agree with the subject.

Example: Le mie amiche sono uscit__: uscit<u>e</u>

1 Francesca e Filippo sono restat__ a casa.
2 Giulia e Susanna non sono uscit__ ieri sera.
3 Nicoletta è andat__ in vacanza.
4 I miei amici sono arrivat__ domenica scorsa.
5 Quando Fabia è entrat__ , ha visto gli amici.
6 Pierluigi non è riuscit__ a finire il lavoro.
7 Professor Rossi, quando è arrivat__?
8 Ti è piaciut__ la partita?
9 Quanto sono costat__ quei libri?
10 Quando è nat__ tua sorella?

Exercise 2

Supply the present perfect of the verb in brackets.

Example: Anna (partire) ieri: è partita

1   Dove (tu comprare) quelle scarpe?
2   Ettore (regalare) un portafoglio a Luisa.
3   Ieri sera (noi andare) a un concerto.
4   Dove (voi trovare) quei fogli?
5   (tu spegnere) la luce?
6   Quanta gente (venire) alla festa?
7   Signora Depaoli, (portare) i documenti?
8   (voi prendere) il giornale?
9   Ieri (io vedere) le mie amiche.
10 Non (tu potere) finire il lavoro?
11 (io dovere) studiare molto per questo esame.
12 Franco (uscire) tardi e (perdere) l'autobus.
13 Chi ti (scrivere) quella lettera?
14 (noi giocare) a pallone tutto il pomeriggio.
15 Federica (cominciare) il nuovo lavoro.
16 Lorenzo non (volere) uscire.
17 Dove (tu mettere) i libri?
18 (tu potere) parlare col professore?
19 (voi avere) tempo per fare tutto?
20 (tu leggere) il giornale di oggi?

Exercise 3

Supply the present perfect of the verb in brackets.

Example: Il dottore (uscire): è uscito

1   (noi dovere) lavorare tutto il giorno.
2   Dove (voi mangiare)?
3   A che ora (tu partire)?
4   Chi (telefonare)?
5   Claudia (volere) restare a casa.
6   (tu conoscere) il fratello di Piero?
7   Silvia (dovere) andare in ospedale.
8   (voi accompagnare) Lina alla stazione?
9   Chi (vincere) il campionato?
10 (tu finire) i compiti?
11 Non (io capire) nulla.
12 (tu portare) i libri in biblioteca?
13 Non (noi riuscire) a finire in tempo.
14 Cosa (voi decidere)?
15 Carla (avere) la febbre.
16 Ugo e Marina non (venire) a cena da noi.
17 Che cosa (voi fare) domenica?
18 Il treno (partire) con mezz'ora di ritardo.
19 La nonna (essere) contenta di vedermi.
20 Chi (tradurre) questo libro?

Exercise 4

Translate into Italian:

1 We've already done this exercise.
2 I haven't finished reading the paper yet.
3 Stefano's never been to Rome.
4 I didn't see Roberto again after the party.
5 Have you [pl.] already paid the bill?
6 Giulia hasn't started working yet.
7 Carlo couldn't work any more.
8 I've never met her parents.
9 Have you [sing.] written the letters already?
10 I've never seen that film.

UNIT THIRTEEN
Direct and indirect object pronouns (2)

1 When a direct object pronoun is used with a verb in the present perfect (or any other compound tense), the past participle must agree in gender and number with the pronoun:

'Hai invitato Anna e Sara?' 'Sì, *le* ho invitat*e*.'	'Did you invite Anna and Sara?' 'Yes, I invited them.'
'Avete portato i libri?' 'Sì, *li* abbiamo portat*i*.'	'Have you brought the books?' 'Yes, we've brought them.'
Ho comprato delle rose e *le* ho dat*e* a Luisa.	I bought some roses and gave them to Luisa.
'Chi ha scritto questa musica?' '*L'*ha scritt*a* Bob Marley.'	'Who wrote this music?' 'Bob Marley wrote it.'
'Dove hai comprato quelle scarpe?' '*Le* ho comprat*e* al mercato.'	'Where did you buy those shoes?' 'I bought them at the market.'
Ho 25 compagni di classe e *li* ho invitat*i* tutti alla mia festa di compleanno.	I have 25 classmates and I've invited all of them to my birthday party.
Non *ci* hanno invitat*i* alla festa.	They didn't invite us to the party. [we are all males, or mixed males and females]
Mauro *mi* ha accompagnat*a* alla stazione.	Mauro took me to the station. [the speaker is female]
Ti hanno invitat*a*?	Did they invite you? [the person addressed is female]

Particular care must be taken when the gender is not shown in the pronoun, as in the last three examples.

Note that when the polite form is used, the past participle always agrees with the feminine pronoun **La**, not with the gender of the person being spoken to:

Signor Belli, chi L'ha invitat*a*?	Who invited you, Mr Belli?
Dottor Ranieri, L'abbiamo vist*a* **ieri sera alla televisione.**	We saw you on television last night, Dr Ranieri.

2 The rule given above does not apply to *indirect* object pronouns: with these, the past participle of the verb never changes:

'Hai telefonato a Anna e Sara?' **'Sì, *gli* ho telefonat*o*.'**	'Did you phone Anna and Sara?' 'Yes, I phoned them.'
Quando è venuta Livia, *le* ho offert*o* un gelato.	When Livia came I offered her an ice cream.
Ho parlato con Carla e *le* ho dett*o* tutto.	I spoke to Carla and told her everything.
Non *ci* hanno scritt*o*.	They didn't write to us.

3 As we saw in Units 7 and 10, when a direct or indirect object pronoun occurs in a sentence together with a verb in the infinitive (usually after **dovere**, **potere**, **volere** or **sapere**), it can be attached to the infinitive.

In these sentences, when the main verb is in the present perfect (or any other compound tense) there is no agreement of the past participle, even with direct object pronouns:

'Hai letto tutti i libri?' 'Sì, ho dovut*o* legger*li* tutti.'	'Did you read all the books?' 'Yes, I had to read all of them.'
Carmen mi ha scritto una lettera, ma non ho ancora potut*o* legger*la*.	Carmen wrote me a letter, but I still haven't been able to read it.
Daniela ha molte compagne di scuola, ma non ha volut*o* invitar*le* alla festa.	Daniela's got a lot of school friends, but she didn't want to/wouldn't ask them to the party.
'Avete fatto gli esercizi?' 'No, non abbiamo saput*o* far*li*.'	'Did you do the exercises?' 'No, we couldn't/didn't know how to do them.'

However, when the direct object pronoun is not attached to the infinitive, the past participle must agree with it:

'Hai letto tutti i libri?' 'Sì, *li* ho dovut*i* leggere tutti.'	'Did you read all the books?' 'Yes, I had to read all of them.'
Carmen mi ha scritto una lettera, ma non *l'*ho ancora potut*a* leggere.	Carmen wrote me a letter but I still haven't been able to read it.
Daniela ha molte compagne di scuola, ma non *le* ha volut*e* invitare alla festa.	Daniela's got a lot of school friends, but she didn't want to/wouldn't ask them to the party.

‘Avete fatto gli esercizi?’ ‘No, non
    li abbiamo saput*i* fare.’

‘Did you do the exercises?’ ‘No, we
couldn't/didn't know how to do
them.’

4 In contemporary spoken Italian (and sometimes in written Italian as well),
agreement of the past participle with first and second person direct object
pronouns tends not to be observed; this is the case with both singular (**mi, ti**) and
plural (**ci, vi**), so quite often you will hear (or read) sentences like the following:

‘Susanna, chi ti ha accompagnato?’
    [instead of *ti* **ha accompagnat*a***]

‘Susanna, who went with/took you?’

‘Mi ha accompagnato Sebastiano.’
    [instead of *mi* **ha accompagnat*a***]

‘Sebastiano went with/took me.’

Ci ha invitato alla festa. [instead of
    ci **ha invitat*i***]

He/She has asked us to the party.

Vi ho visto entrare al cinema.
    [instead of *vi* **ho vist*i***]

I saw you go into the cinema.

However, the agreement is always made with the third person pronouns (**lo,
la, li, le**):

L'ha accompagnat*a* Sebastiano.

Sebastiano went with/took her.

Li ho invitat*i* alla festa.

I've asked them to the party.

‘Quando hai visto Carla e Livia?’
    ‘*Le* ho vist*e* ieri.’

‘When did you see Carla and Livia?’ ‘I
saw them yesterday.’

Exercise 1

Complete the sentences with the direct object pronouns, making sure that the
past participle agrees.

Example: Ho visto Gianna e _____ ho invitat__: l'ho invitat<u>a</u>

1 Ho comprato dei fiori e _____ ho mess__ in un vaso.
2 La zia è partita e _____ ho accompagnat__alla stazione.
3 Ho visto delle belle scarpe e _____ho comprat__.
4 Lara ha aperto le finestre, ma Luca _____ ha chius__.
5 Mi hanno regalato dei biscotti e _____ ho mangiat__ tutti.
6 Luisa, non hai sentito che Claudio _____ ha chiamat__?
7 Gaetano ha preso il giornale e _____ha lett__.
8 ‘Vi hanno invitati alla festa?’ ‘No, non _____ hanno invitat__.’
9 ‘Hai preso i biglietti per il concerto?’ ‘Sì, _____ ho pres__.’
10 Cerchi i libri? _____ ho dat__ a Giovanni.

Exercise 2

Complete the sentences with the correct direct or indirect object pronoun, making sure that the past participle agrees where necessary.

Examples: Non ho telefonato a Maria, _____ ho scritt__: le ho scritto;
Ho comprato una minigonna rossa e __ho indossat__ per la festa: l'ho indossata

1 Ho incontrato Lina e ____ ho offert__ un caffè.
2 Cerco Paola e Gianni, ____ avete vist__?
3 Non ho la bicicletta perchè ____ho imprestat__ a Filippo.
4 Non ho scritto a Paola, ____ ho telefonat__.
5 Dove sono le chiavi? Chi ____ ha pres__?
6 Parlo bene l'italiano e il tedesco perché ____ ho studiat__ per sette anni.
7 Ieri ho visto Alessandro e ____ ha presentat__ sua sorella.
8 Caterina, chi ____ ha accompagnat__ ieri sera?
9 Oggi è il compleanno di Daniela, ____ hai mandat__ gli auguri?
10 Gianna è una vecchia amica: ____ho conosciut__ otto anni fa.
11 'Dove avete lasciato la bici?' '____abbiamo lasciat__ in strada.'
12 Hai telefonato a Giacomo? Che cosa ____ hai dett__?
13 'Hai comprato i francobolli?' 'Sì, ____ ho comprat__.'
14 Signora, L'ho cercata ieri, ma non ____ho trovat__.
15 Sebastiano ha molte amiche e io ____ ho conosciut__ tutte.
16 'Cosa hai detto a Matteo?' 'Non ____ ho dett__ nulla.'
17 'Chi ha pagato il conto?' '____ha pagat__ mia madre.'
18 'Cosa hai raccontato a Giulia?' '____ ho raccontat__ la verità.'
19 Professore, chi ____ha accompagnat__ in aeroporto?
20 Questa è una rivista molto interessante: ____ho lett__ tutta.

Exercise 3

Rewrite the sentences as shown in the example.

Example: Ho dovuto comprarle: Le ho dovute comprare.

1 Non ho saputo farli.
2 Ho voluto vederli.
3 Non abbiamo potuto chiamarlo.
4 Hanno potuto aiutarvi?
5 Abbiamo dovuto invitarla.
6 Non ha saputo tradurle.
7 Avete dovuto accompagnarle?
8 Ha voluto mangiarla.
9 Hai potuto vederli?
10 Non hanno voluto farle.

Exercise 4

Translate into Italian.

1 Sabina hasn't invited me [f].
2 Who called you [fs]?
3 We phoned them yesterday.
4 I looked for you [mp], but I didn't find you.
5 Chiara took us to the bus stop.
6 I sent you [pl.] a postcard – did you receive it?
7 My grandparents gave me 100 euros, but I've already spent it. [Say: 'spent them']
8 I bought two rolls and ate them.
9 'Have you [sing.] switched the light off?' 'Yes, I've switched it off.'
10 Carla hasn't been able to help them [f].

UNIT FOURTEEN
Direct and indirect object pronouns
(3: stressed forms)

1 Direct and indirect object pronouns do not only have the unstressed (or weak) forms that we saw in Units 7, 10 and 13: they also have *stressed* (or strong) forms:

Direct object stressed forms	*Indirect object stressed forms*
me	**a me**
te	**a te**
lui/lei/Lei*	**a lui/a lei/a Lei***
noi	**a noi**
voi	**a voi**
loro/Loro*	**a loro/a Loro***

* As usual, the pronoun **Lei** (third person singular feminine) and the pronoun **Loro** (third person plural) are used for the formal form.

2 The stressed forms of direct object and indirect object pronouns are used to give emphasis to the pronoun or to stress a contrast; unlike unstressed forms, they normally come after the verb, except when used with the verbs **piacere, sembrare, servire, bastare, parere** and **mancare** (see Unit 11). Stressed forms always refer to people, not objects:

Chiamo *voi*, non *loro*.	I'm calling/phoning you, not them.
Vedo *lei*, ma non vedo *lui*.	I can see her, but I can't see him.
Aspetto Francesco, non *te*.	I'm waiting for Francesco, not you.
Invito solo *te*.	I'm only inviting *you*.
Invito solo *Lei*, Signor Paoli.	I'm only inviting *you*, Mr Paoli.
***A me* non piace il caffè.**	*I* don't like coffee.
***A me* sembra giusto.**	*I* think it's fair/It seems fair to *me*.
Telefono *a te*, ma non *a loro*.	I'll phone you, but not them.
Billy scrive *a noi* e non ai suoi genitori.	Billy writes to us and not his parents.
Devi rendere i soldi *a me*, non a mio fratello.	You've got to give *me* the money, not my brother.

Note the difference between the two sentences 'Non mi piace il caffè' and 'A me non piace il caffè'. The first simply states that I don't like coffee, while the second puts the emphasis on the pronoun 'me', implying that there are people who do like coffee but I am not one of them. The same applies to the sentences 'Mi sembra giusto' and 'A me sembra giusto': the second sentence stresses the fact that there are other people who *don't* think it's fair.

3 As the above examples suggest, stressed direct and indirect object pronouns *cannot be used to refer to objects*. When referring to objects, the noun has to be repeated (as is also generally the case in English):

'Prendi la frutta e il dolce?' 'Prendo la frutta, ma non il dolce.' [Not **'Prendo lei, ma non lui.'**]	'Are you having the fruit and the sweet?' 'I'm having the fruit, but not the sweet.'
'Porti la chitarra e i CD?' 'Porto i CD ma non la chitarra.' [Not **'Porto loro ma non lei.'**]	'Are you bringing the guitar and the CDs?' 'I'll bring the CDs, but not the guitar.' [or, at a pinch, 'I'll bring *them*, but not *it*.']

4 The stressed forms of the object pronouns are used after all prepositions (see Unit 8), not just **a**. This is true even when no emphasis is required:

Vengo con Lei, Signora.	I'm coming with you(, Madam).
Chi di loro non vuole venire?	Which of them doesn't want to come?
Puoi dormire da me, stasera.	You can sleep at my place tonight.
Faccio questo per te.	I'm doing this for you.
Puoi contare su di me.*	You can count on me.
Dopo di te* ci sono io.	After you it's me/my turn.
Non ho nulla contro di voi.*	I've got nothing against you.

* When **su**, **sopra**, **dopo**, **contro** are used with a personal pronoun, the pronoun is preceded by the preposition **di** (see Unit 8, paragraphs 9, 20).

5 The stressed forms are also always used when the verb has two pronoun direct or indirect objects, even where no emphasis is required:

Ho visto te e lui in città. [not **Ti e lo ho visto in città.**]	I saw you and him in town.
Invito voi e loro. [not **Vi e li invito.**]	I'm inviting you and them.
Scrive a te e a me. [not **Ti e mi scrive.**]	He writes to you and me.
Regaliamo fiori a loro e a lei. [not **Gli e le regaliamo fiori.**]	We're giving flowers to them and her.

6 Stressed forms are always used after **anche/pure** (also, too), **neanche/ nemmeno/neppure** (not even, neither), **come** (as, like), **quanto** (as much as), **eccetto (che)*/meno (che)*/tranne (che)*/salvo (che)*** (except, but):

Invito anche voi.	I'm inviting *you* as well.
Devi fare come me.	You should do as I do/do it like me.
Maria lavora quanto te.	Maria works as much as you (do).
Devi chiedere anche a noi.	You have to ask *us* as well.
Non credo neppure a lui.	I don't believe *him* either.
Vengono tutti meno lui.	They're all coming except him/ Everyone but him's coming.
Faccio questo per tutti meno che* per lei.	I'm doing/I'll do this for everyone except/but her.
Anna telefona a tutti salvo che* a loro.	Anna phones everyone except/but them.
Sandro esce con tutti salvo che* con noi.	Sandro goes out with everybody except/but us.
Sono tutti contro di noi.	They are all against us.

* The forms **eccetto che/meno che/tranne che/salvo che** are used when there is a preposition before the pronoun.

7 Note that when the stressed forms of the direct object pronouns are used in a sentence with the verb in a compound tense (see Unit 13, paragraph 1), the past participle does not agree with the pronoun:

Ho chiamato voi, non loro.	I called *you*, not them.
Ho visto lei, ma non ho visto lui.	I saw *her*, but I didn't see him.
Lucia ha invitato loro, ma non lui.	Lucia has invited *them*, but not him.

Exercise 1

Replace the English words with the correct Italian ones.

Examples: Mario chiama (them), non (you [pl.]): loro, voi; La nonna ha dato i soldi a (you [sing.]) e non a (me): te, me

1 Prima accompagno (her) a scuola, poi (you [sing.]) in palestra.
2 Dovete invitare anche (them).
3 Non è venuto nessuno, nemmeno (her).
4 Hanno invitato (us) e non (you [pl.])?!
5 All'esame hanno promosso tutti tranne (me).
6 Credo a tutti meno che a (him).

7 Carla vuole bene a (me) quanto a (you [sing.]).
8 A (you [polite]) credo, Professore.
9 Voglio presentare i miei amici anche a (you [pl.]).
10 A (her), come a (them), non sembra giusto.

Exercise 2

Translate the following sentences, where necessary underlining the emphasised words.

Examples: Dovete invitare anche me: You should invite me as well/too; A
me manca il sole, a te no?: I'm missing the sun – aren't you? or
I miss the sun – don't you?

1 Nessuno suona la batteria come me.
2 Tutti gli studenti hanno fatto il compito meno lui.
3 Sergio chiama te, non me.
4 Accompagno anche te.
5 Capisco quanto te.
6 Mauro dice la verità a tutti, tranne che a me.
7 Dovete telefonare anche a me.
8 Claudia impresta i dischi a noi, non a voi.
9 Do il mio indirizzo a tutti salvo che a lei.
10 Regalo un libro a lei e un disco a lui.

Exercise 3

Replace the English words with the correct Italian ones, as you did in Exercise 1.

1 Chi di (you [pl.]) non può venire alla festa?
2 All'esame orale sono passato subito dopo di (him).
3 Sopra di (them) abita una signora molto gentile.
4 Abbiamo deciso fra (us).
5 Esci con (her) anche stasera?

Exercise 4

Translate into Italian, using the stressed form of the pronouns:

1   Everyone's against me!
2   Are you [sing.] coming with me?
3   I've bought a present for you [sing.].
4   You [sing.] can't count on him.
5   Can I sleep at your [pl.] place tonight?

UNIT FIFTEEN
Relative pronouns

1 The Italian relative pronouns correspond to the English 'who', 'which', 'that', 'whom', 'whose'. They have two forms: invariable (**che**, **cui**) and variable (**il quale** [ms], **la quale** [fs], **i quali** [mp], **le quali** [fp]):

Il treno *che* **prendo la mattina è sempre molto affollato.**	The train (that) I get in the morning is always very crowded.
La storia *che* **ho letto è strana.**	The story (that) I've read is strange.
La ragazza *che/la quale* **ha telefonato ha bisogno di un favore.**	The girl who phoned needs a favour.
Gli amici *che/i quali* **sono venuti a trovarmi sono irlandesi.**	The friends who came to see me are Irish.
Hai ancora le chiavi *che* **ti ho dato?**	Have you still got the keys (that) I gave you?
Il ragazzo *con cui/col quale* **esci è molto simpatico.**	The boy with whom you are going out/ you're going out with is very nice.
La ragazza *a cui/alla quale* **ho dato i libri è una mia amica.**	The girl to whom I gave the books/I gave the books to is a friend of mine.

The invariable forms, which can replace all nouns (masculine, feminine, singular, plural) are the most frequently used.

2 The invariable form **che** is used for masculine, feminine, singular and plural nouns; it can be either a subject or a direct object:

Il gruppo *che* [subject, ms] **suona stasera è molto conosciuto.***	The group who are playing tonight are very well known.
Il cantante *che* [direct object, ms] **abbiamo sentito ieri sera non è molto bravo.**	The singer (whom) we heard last night isn't very good.
Le scarpe *che* [direct object, fp] **ho comprato sono care.**	The shoes (that) I bought are expensive.

Non conosco i ragazzi *che* [subject, mp] **sono appena arrivati.**	I don't know the boys who have just arrived.

* In Italian, collective nouns (e.g. **il gruppo**, 'the group', **la squadra**, 'the squad/team') are always followed by the singular of the verb, never the plural.

3 When a preposition is needed before the invariable relative pronoun (e.g. if it stands for an indirect object), the form used is **cui**:

Lo zio *a cui* **scrivo sempre arriva domani.**	The uncle I always write to/to whom I always write is arriving tomorrow.
La vicina *per cui* **ho fatto la spesa mi ha invitato a cena.**	The neighbour I went shopping for/for whom I went shopping has invited me to dinner.
Non conosci la persona (*a*) *cui* **devo telefonare.***	You don't know the person (that) I have to phone.
Il dentista *da cui* **vado è molto bravo.**	The dentist I go to is very good.
Nella città *in cui* **abito ci sono molti cinema.**	There are a lot of cinemas in the town in which I live.
Gli amici *con cui* **esco sono italiani.**	The friends I go out with are Italian.
Non capisco la ragione *per cui* **Paola non è venuta.****	I don't understand (the reason) why Paola didn't come.
Non ho ancora letto le notizie *di cui* **parli.**	I haven't read the news you're talking about yet.

* The preposition **a** can sometimes be omitted before **cui**.
** The Italian for 'the reason/reasons why' is always **la ragione/le ragioni per cui**, never **perché**.

4 The variable forms **il quale** [ms], **la quale** [fs], **i quali** [mp], **le quali** [fp] are used as subject, indirect object and – very rarely – as direct object. They must agree in gender and number with the noun they replace:

Paolo, *il quale* **è sempre in ritardo, non è ancora arrivato.**	Paolo, who is always late, still hasn't arrived.
Ho parlato con una ragazza *la quale* **mi ha dato tutte le informazioni.**	I spoke to a girl who gave me all the information.
Tullio e Anna sono amici *i quali* **mi invitano spesso.**	Tullio and Anna are friends who often invite me round.
Ci sono due signore *le quali* **non hanno prenotato.**	There are two ladies who haven't booked.
L'amica con *la quale* **sono andata in vacanza si chiama Elisa.**	The friend with whom I went on holiday/I went away with is called Elisa.

Questa è l'amica *della* quale* ti ho parlato.	This is the friend I told you about.
L'insegnante *al* quale* ho parlato è stato molto gentile.	The teacher I spoke to was very kind.

* Remember to combine the definite article with the preposition (see Unit 8, paragraph 2) when using the variable forms.

5 When a relative pronoun is preceded by **in** or **a**, and these denote place, it is often replaced, in contemporary Italian, by the adverb **dove**. **Da dove** or **di dove** can be used when the relative pronoun is preceded by the preposition **da**:

Milano è la città dove [for **in cui**] **vive Walter.**	Milan is the city where Walter lives.
Questo è il negozio dove [for **in cui**] **lavora Pia.**	This is the shop where Pia works.
La stazione dove [for **a cui**] **deve andare non è lontana da qui.**	The station he's got to go to isn't far from here.
La scuola da dove/di dove [for **da cui**] **viene Enrico è molto buona.**	The school Enrico went to [lit. comes from] is very good.

6 The relative pronouns (both variable and invariable) can be used in conjunction with the demonstrative pronouns **colui** and **quello**.

Colui can only refer to people. It has three forms: **colui** [ms], **colei** [fs], **coloro** [mp and fp]; these combine with **che/cui** or **il quale/la quale/i quali/le quali** as follows:

colui che or **colui il quale**	he who
colei che or **colei la quale**	she who
coloro che or **coloro i quali/coloro le quali**	those who

Quello has four forms: **quello** [ms], **quella** [fs], **quelli** [mp], **quelle** [fp]; these only combine with **che/cui**, and can refer to both objects and people:

quello che	that which, he who, the one which/who
quella che	that which, she who, the one which/who
quelli che	those which, those who, the ones which/who
quelle che	those which, those who, the ones which/who

The use of **quello che** etc. to refer to a person is rather informal, unlike **colui che/colui il quale** etc. which are quite formal.

Colui che pensa questo sbaglia.	He who thinks this is wrong.
Quello che pensa questo sbaglia.	Anyone who thinks this is wrong.
Possono entrare solo *coloro che/ coloro i quali* hanno l'invito.	Only those who have an invitation may come/go in.
Possono entrare solo *quelli che* hanno l'invito.	Only people with an invitation can come/go in.
Coloro a cui/ai quali scrivo sono amici di mio fratello.	Those I'm writing to are friends of my brother('s).
Quelli a cui scrivo sono amici di mio fratello.	The people I'm writing to are friends of my brother('s).
Quelli che sono sul tavolo sono i libri di Tullio.	Those/The ones (which are) on the table are Tullio's books.
Ci sono due case: *quella in cui* abita Giorgio è la più grande.	There are two houses: the one Giorgio lives in is the bigger.

7 When referring to people, the pronoun **chi** (who, anyone who, the person/ people who) is often used instead of the more formal 'double relative' (**colui/ colei/coloro che, colui il quale**, etc.). **Chi** is always used with the verb in the third person singular; past participles and adjectives are always in the masculine singular:

Chi pensa questo sbaglia.	Anyone who thinks this is wrong.
Può entrare solo *chi* ha l'invito.	Only people who have an invitation can come in/go in.
Non ho visto *chi* è entrato.	I didn't see who came in/went in.
Esco con *chi* mi invita.	I'll go out with anyone who invites/asks me.
Lavoro per *chi* mi paga.	I'll work for anyone who pays me.
Ripeto la spiegazione per *chi* non ha capito.	I'll repeat the explanation for those/ anyone who didn't understand.
Hai risposto a *chi* ti ha scritto?	Have you replied to the person/people who wrote to you?

Exercise 1

Complete the sentences with the relative pronouns **che** or **cui**.

Examples: La ragazza ____ ho invitato è mia cugina: <u>che</u>; Il ragazzo a ____ devo telefonare è Matteo: <u>cui</u>

1 Il film ____ mi hai consigliato è molto bello.
2 La palestra in ____ vado non è lontana.

3 I bambini ____ sono venuti sono i miei cugini.
4 Non conosco le persone con ____ esci.
5 La torta ____ ha fatto tua mamma è molto buona.
6 Quando mi rendi i CD ____ ti ho imprestato?
7 L'argomento di ____ parla Paolo non mi interessa.
8 La ragione per ____ non siamo venuti è semplice.
9 La città in ____ sono nato non è molto grande.
10 Come è andato l'esame ____ hai dato ieri?

Exercise 2

Complete the sentences with the relative pronouns **che** or **cui**.

Examples: Hai comprato le cose ____ ti ho chiesto?: <u>che</u>; La discoteca
in ____ andiamo è in centro: <u>cui</u>

1 Nella biblioteca in ____ vado a studiare fa sempre freddo.
2 Gli amici da ____ siamo andati sono molto simpatici.
3 La stanza in ____ dorme Luigi è la più luminosa.
4 Non mi piace la musica ____ ascolti tu.
5 Hai già letto il libro ____ ti hanno regalato?
6 Gli esercizi ____ avete fatto sono tutti giusti.
7 Quello è il muro su ____ vogliamo mettere i poster.
8 Vuoi leggere la lettera ____ mi ha scritto Angela?
9 Il medico da ____ vanno i miei genitori è molto giovane.
10 Di chi è la bici con ____ sei arrivato?

Exercise 3

Replace **che** and **cui** with **il quale**, **la quale**, **i quali** or **le quali** (remember to combine the definite article and the preposition, where necessary).

Example: Gli amici da cui andiamo in vacanza sono simpatici: dai quali

1 Mia madre, che è infermiera, lavora in un ospedale.
2 Chi è la ragazza con cui sei uscito?
3 Gli esami di cui ha parlato il professore sono a giugno.
4 Il campeggio in cui siamo stati è vicino al mare.
5 Tutte le ragazze a cui ho telefonato hanno accettato l'invito.
6 Franco, che è un bravo attore, ha trovato lavoro in un teatro.
7 Il parrucchiere da cui vado è un amico.
8 Le cugine di Chiara, che abitano vicino a me, sono simpatiche.

9 Le amiche di cui ti ho parlato arrivano domani.
10 I nostri amici, che sono tutti italiani, non parlano inglese.

Exercise 4

Supply the correct double relative pronoun (**colui/colei/coloro che**).

Example: _____ hanno biglietti possono entrare: <u>coloro che</u>

1   _____ ha scritto questo libro è la sorella di Piero.
2   _____ ci hanno invitati sono amici di Luisa.
3   _____ ha vinto il premio è Antonio.
4   _____ dà le informazioni deve parlare inglese e spagnolo.
5   _____ hanno parlato sono persone molto importanti.

Exercise 5

Complete using the correct pronouns (**chi** or **quello/quella/quelli/quelle che**).

Examples: ____ non ha il biglietto non entra: <u>chi</u>; ____ hai fatto non sono errori gravi: <u>quelli che</u>

1 Non conosco ____ ha scritto questa lettera.
2 La spiegazione è ____ ti ho dato.
3 Il controllore è ____ controlla i biglietti.
4 Vince il premio ____ finisce per primo.
5 ____ ti ho imprestato sono i libri che devi leggere.
6 ____ abbiamo comprato è un'auto economica.
7 ____ fa la spesa al mercato spende meno.
8 ____ abbiamo prenotato è un hotel di lusso.
9 ____ non può venire deve telefonare per avvertire.
10 ____ ho visto in quel negozio sono scarpe molto belle.

Exercise 6

Translate into Italian:

1 The book which I want to buy is too expensive.
2 The lady I spoke to is German.
3 The people who phoned live in America!
4 The town I live in isn't very big.

5 Anyone who wants to go to university must be able to read and write.
6 Paolo, who's lost his mobile, is not happy.
7 I like that song, but I prefer the ones we heard last night.
8 This is Fabio's sister, who lent me her bike.
9 Did you [sing.] see who ate the peaches?
10 Who's the man you [pl.] sold the tickets to?

UNIT SIXTEEN
The imperfect tense

1 The imperfect is, together with the present perfect, one of the most used past tenses in Italian. It is called 'imperfect' because, generally speaking, there is no reference to the beginning or end of the action it expresses: either the length of time the action lasted is not relevant, or the action is seen as the background to another action, or two actions took place at the same time and lasted the same length of time. Here are some typical examples:

Mio nonno *lavorava* in India.	My grandfather used to work in India.
Mia nonna *era* infermiera.	My grandmother was a nurse.
Mentre io *entravo*, Elena *usciva*.	As I was going in, Elena was coming out.
Quando ho cominciato la scuola *avevo* cinque anni.	When I started school I was five.
Elena è arrivata mentre io *uscivo*.	Elena arrived as I was going out.
Claudia *parlava* con un'amica quando è arrivato l'autobus.	Claudia was talking to a friend when the bus arrived.
Quando *ero* al mare *nuotavo* tutti i giorni.	When I was at the seaside I went/used to go swimming every day.

As you can see from the examples, the Italian imperfect corresponds to several different English forms. We will look at the different meanings and uses of this tense, but first we will look at its forms.

The forms of the imperfect

2 The forms of the imperfect are very regular. Here are the endings for the three conjugations (**-are, -ere, -ire**):

	-are	*-ere*	*-ire*
(io)	**-avo**	**-evo**	**-ivo**
(tu)	**-avi**	**-evi**	**-ivi**
(lui/lei)	**-ava**	**-eva**	**-iva**
(noi)	**-avamo**	**-evamo**	**-ivamo**
(voi)	**-avate**	**-evate**	**-ivate**
(loro)	**-avano**	**-evano**	**-ivano**

Regular verbs ending in **-are** are conjugated as follows:

Parlare	*To speak*
parlavo	I spoke/was speaking/used to speak
parlavi	you spoke/were speaking/used to speak
parlava	he/she/it spoke/was speaking/used to speak
parlavamo	we spoke/were speaking/used to speak
parlavate	you spoke/were speaking/used to speak
parlavano	they spoke/were speaking/used to speak

Regular verbs ending in **-ere** are conjugated as follows:

Prendere	*To take*/get
prendevo	I took/was taking/used to take
prendevi	you took/were taking/used to take
prendeva	he/she/it took/was taking/used to take
prendevamo	we took/were taking/used to take
prendevate	you took/were taking/used to take
prendevano	they took/were taking/used to take

The verb **avere** also follows this same regular pattern:

avevo	I had/was having/used to have
avevi	you had/were having/used to have
aveva	he/she/it had/was having/used to have
avevamo	we had/were having/used to have
avevate	you had/were having/used to have
avevano	they had/were having/used to have

Regular verbs ending in **-ire** are conjugated as follows:

Partire	*To leave*
partivo	I left/was leaving/used to leave
partivi	you left/were leaving/used to leave
partiva	he/she/it left/was leaving/used to leave
partivamo	we left/were leaving/used to leave
partivate	you left/were leaving/used to leave
partivano	they left/were leaving/used to leave

Mio nonno parlava molto bene l'italiano.	My grandfather spoke Italian very well.
Mentre prendevamo il caffè è suonato il telefono.	While we were having coffee the telephone rang.
Quando Carla aveva 5 anni abitava a Roma.	When Carla was five she lived in Rome.
Sono arrivato quando il treno partiva.	I arrived as the train was leaving.
Mio fratello andava a scuola in autobus.	My brother used to go to school by bus.
Di solito Gianni e sua sorella andavano al cinema insieme.	Usually Gianni and his sister went to the cinema together.
Quando Maurizio lavorava in quel supermercato lo pagavano pochissimo.	When Maurizio worked in that supermarket they paid him very little.
Mentre Sebastiano leggeva il giornale, io ho finito i compiti.	While Sebastiano was reading the paper I finished my homework.

3 Not many verbs are irregular in the imperfect. **Essere** is one:

ero	I was/used to be
eri	you were/used to be
era	he/she/it was/used to be
eravamo	we were/used to be
eravate	you were/used to be
erano	they were/used to be

Like the present, the imperfect of **essere** can be used with the pronoun **ci** (see Unit 4): **c'era** (there was), **c'erano** (there were).

Other irregular verbs are **bere**, **dire** and **fare**:

bevevo	I drank/was drinking/used to drink
bevevi	you drank/were drinking/used to drink
beveva	he/she/it drank/was drinking/used to drink
bevevamo	we drank/were drinking/used to drink
bevevate	you drank/were drinking/used to drink
bevevano	they drank/were drinking/used to drink

dicevo	I said/was saying/used to say
dicevi	you said/were saying/used to say
diceva	he/she/it said/was saying/used to say
dicevamo	we said/were saying/used to say
dicevate	you said/were saying/used to say
dicevano	they said/were saying/used to say

facevo	I did/was doing/used to do
facevi	you did/were doing/used to do
faceva	he/she/it did/was doing/used to do
facevamo	we did/were doing/used to do
facevate	you did/were doing/used to do
facevano	they did/were doing/used to do

All verbs ending in **-urre** have the following pattern:

-u*cevo*	**trad*ucevo***	I translated/was translating/used to translate
-u*cevi*	**trad*ucevi***	you translated/were translating/used to translate
-u*ceva*	**trad*uceva***	he/she/it translated/was translating/used to translate
-u*cevamo*	**trad*ucevamo***	we translated/were translating/used to translate
-u*cevate*	**trad*ucevate***	you translated/were translating/used to translate
-u*cevano*	**trad*ucevano***	they translated/were translating/used to translate

Quando ero bambino abitavo a Parma.	When I was a child I lived in Parma.
Ieri il tempo era bello.	Yesterday the weather was lovely.
Al concerto c'erano più di 900 persone.	There were more than 900 people at the concert.
Mia sorella beveva solo acqua minerale, ora beve anche acqua di rubinetto.	My sister only used to drink mineral water, now she drinks tap water as well.
Cosa dicevi?	What were you saying?
Cosa faceva, Signora, quando non lavorava?	What did you do(, Madam), when you weren't working/didn't work?
L'interprete traduceva, ma nessuno ascoltava.	The interpreter was translating, but nobody was listening.

Negative form

4 The negative is formed, as usual, by putting **non** before the verb:

Di solito la domenica non uscivo.	I didn't usually go out on Sundays.
Quando hai telefonato non facevo niente di speciale.	When you phoned I wasn't doing anything special.

Use of the imperfect

5 The imperfect is used for descriptions of situations in the past, when it is not necessary (or important) to say how long an action lasted. This generally happens with verbs like **essere**, **sembrare** and **avere**, and with verbs expressing will, desire or intention, possibility or ability; but it can happen with other verbs as well:

C'erano molte persone che aspettavano il treno.	There were a lot of people (who were) waiting for the train.
Ieri sera sembravi molto stanco.	You looked very tired last night.
Mia nonna era molto alta e aveva i capelli bianchi.	My grandmother was very tall and had white hair.
Faceva freddo, in montagna?	Was it cold in the mountains?
Cosa volevi?	What did you want/were you wanting?
Due anni fa abitavo a Milano.	Two years ago I was living in Milan.
Suo padre era medico.	His father was a doctor.

6 The imperfect is also used to express actions which were habitual or happened repeatedly in the past:

L'estate scorsa giocavamo sempre a tennis.	Last summer we played tennis all the time.
Quando ero in vacanza andavo al cinema tutti i giorni.	When I was on holiday I went to the cinema every day.
Tutte le mattine a colazione Giulia prendeva solo del caffè.	Every morning Giulia just had coffee for breakfast.
Cenavamo alle otto.	We used to have dinner at eight.

7 Since the imperfect is used when it is not relevant how long the action lasted, it is not used when it is stated how many times, or for how long, something happened:

L'estate scorsa sono andato al cinema *25 volte*.	Last summer I went to the cinema 25 times.
Ha fatto molto freddo *per due giorni*.	It was very cold for two days.
Giulia ha lavorato qui *da gennaio a giugno*.	Giulia worked here from January to June.
Ho abitato a Milano *per due anni*.	I lived in Milan for two years.
Ieri abbiamo lavorato *tutto il giorno*.	Yesterday we worked all day.
Ieri sono stato in biblioteca *dalle nove alle undici*.	Yesterday I was in the library from nine till 11.

8 When a sentence refers to two or more events which happened in the past, it is helpful to think in terms of 'foreground' and 'background', as in these two English examples: 'While I was doing the dishes [continuous background], I heard [foreground] the doorbell'; 'I saw [foreground] Juve a couple of times when I was [continuous background] in Turin'. In Italian, in cases like these, the imperfect expresses the continuous 'background' action against which the 'foreground' action is seen to occur:

Mentre* dormivate ho preparato la colazione.	While you were sleeping/asleep I prepared breakfast.
Mia madre ha conosciuto mio padre quando abitava a Firenze.	My mother met my father when she was living in Florence.
Mauro non ha preso l'ombrello anche se pioveva.	Mauro didn't take the umbrella even though it was raining.
Marco ha telefonato quando eravate al cinema.	Marco phoned when you were at the cinema.
Non sono uscita perché pioveva.	I didn't go out because it was raining.

* Note that **mentre** (while), in the past, is always followed by the imperfect.

If the two events happened at the same time and lasted for the same length of time, then both verbs are in the imperfect:

Mentre noi facevamo il compito di matematica, Carla ripassava filosofia.	While we were doing our maths homework, Carla was revising philosophy.
Mentre Alessandro preparava la cena, Claudia leggeva il giornale.	While Alessandro was preparing dinner, Claudia was reading the newspaper.
Quando io lavoravo al supermercato, mia sorella lavorava in un cinema.	When I worked in the supermarket, my sister worked in a cinema.
Il gatto miagolava perché aveva fame.	The cat was miaowing because it was hungry.

Exercise 1

Supply the imperfect of the verb in brackets.

Example: Silvio (lavorare) molto: lavorava

1 Il nonno di Piero (parlare) sei lingue.
2 Laura (passare) sempre l'estate al mare.
3 Che lavoro (fare) tua nonna?
4 Mentre (io studiare), Maria (riposare).
5 Il treno (partire) sempre in ritardo.
6 Dove (lavorare) Nicola?
7 Paolo non (dire) mai la verità.
8 Ieri (fare) freddo.
9 Da bambini (noi abitare) in campagna.
10 (voi essere) stanchi ieri sera?
11 (loro andare) in piscina tutti i giorni.
12 Lei (essere) infermiera, Signora?
13 Non (noi uscire) mai di domenica.
14 (tu sapere) la verità?
15 (io conoscere) bene suo cugino.
16 Paolo (amare) Francesca.
17 (voi dormire) ancora?
18 I miei amici (essere) studenti.
19 (tu avere) fame?
20 (loro dovere) partire.

Exercise 2

Supply the correct tense (present perfect or imperfect) of the verb in brackets.

Examples: (io comprare) la macchina due anni fa: ho comprato; D'estate (noi andare) in spiaggia ogni mattina: andavamo

1 Elena, a che ora (tu partire) ieri?
2 Chi (essere) Dante Alighieri?
3 (io studiare) per due ore.
4 Di solito (noi mangiare) in mensa.
5 Claudia (rimanere) in casa tutto il giorno.
6 Mia nonna (avere) gli occhi azzurri.
7 Nicoletta e Luigina non (sembrare) sorelle.
8 Ieri Andrea (spendere) 150 euro.
9 Signora, dove (andare) in vacanza l'anno scorso?
10 I loro amici (essere) sempre allegri.

Exercise 3

Supply the correct tense (present perfect or imperfect) of the verbs in brackets.

   Example: Mentre (noi guardare) la televisione Isabella (ascoltare) la radio: guardavamo, ascoltava

1 Marco (arrivare) tardi perché il treno (essere) in ritardo.
2 (io conoscere) Susanna quando (io abitare) a Napoli.
3 Quanti anni (tu avere) quando (tu cominciare) a lavorare?
4 Sergio (telefonare) proprio mentre (io fare) il bagno.
5 Anna e Giacomo (venire) a piedi perché l'auto (essere) guasta.
6 Non (loro fare) la spesa perché non (loro sapere) cosa comprare.
7 Cosa (loro dire) quando (loro vedere) Gianni ieri sera?
8 Massimo non (venire) alla festa perché (avere) mal di testa.
9 (noi arrivare) alla stazione proprio mentre il treno (partire).
10 (io imprestare) la bici a Giulia perché la sua (essere) rotta.

Exercise 4

Put the text into a past tense, changing the verbs in italics to either the present perfect or the imperfect.

Sabato sera in un locale del centro *suona* un gruppo rock che *piace* molto a Massimo, così i miei amici e io *decidiamo* di andare a questo concerto. *Arriviamo* davanti al locale con molto anticipo: *mancano* tre ore all'inizio, ma *ci sono* già molte persone. Massimo *è* molto impaziente. Dopo una mezz'ora, mentre *aspettiamo*, *sentiamo* suonare il cellulare di Massimo e lui *risponde*. *Vediamo* che Massimo *è* preoccupato e quando *finisce* di parlare ci *spiega*. *È* suo padre che lo *chiama* perché *ha* bisogno di aiuto: la sua auto *è* guasta e non *sa* come tornare a casa. Massimo *parte* subito per andare a prenderlo e accompagnarlo a casa anche se *ha* paura di perdere il concerto. Per fortuna, però, Massimo *riesce* a tornare dopo un'ora, proprio mentre *aprono* le porte.

Exercise 5

Translate into Italian:

1 How long did you [sing.] spend in Bologna?
2 We went to the cinema last night.
3 You [pl.] seemed happy.

4 Gemma's father was a sailor.
5 Claudia and Monica didn't come on holiday with us this time.
6 My parents usually went out at eight.
7 My father worked in India for three years.
8 What time did you [pl.] get the bus yesterday morning?
9 Last year we did gym on Monday mornings.
10 Where did you [sing.] buy those shoes?
11 I didn't call you [sing.] because you were asleep.
12 When you [pl.] were living in London, I was living in Paris.
13 How old was Susanna when she went to university?
14 While I was watching the television, Anna came in and switched it off.
15 Paolo and Giulia didn't come because Paolo was too tired.

UNIT SEVENTEEN
The pronouns **ne** and **ci**

The pronoun *ne*

1 The pronoun **ne** is used to refer to a part of a whole, corresponding to 'of it/-them', as in 'some of it/them', 'two of them', etc. It is normally used together with quantities, whether expressed in numbers or in any other way (kilos, litres, metres, slices, cups, 'too much/little', 'enough', etc.); it is always placed before the verb:

La torta era molto buona e *ne* ho mangiate due fette.	The cake was very good, and I ate two slices (of it).
'Quanti fratelli hai?' '*Ne* ho due.'	'How many brothers and sisters do you have?' 'I have two (of them).'
'Ha degli euro, Signor Watt?' 'Sì, *ne* ho 50.'	'Have you got any euros, Mr Watt?' 'Yes, I've got 50 (of them).'
'Hai tutti i CD di Frank Zappa?' 'No, *ne* ho solo tre.'	'Have you got all Frank Zappa's CDs?' 'No, I've only got three (of them).'
'Mangi la frutta?' 'Sì, *ne* mangio molta.'	'Do you eat fruit?' 'Yes, I eat a lot (of it).'
'Hai abbastanza soldi?' 'Sì, ne ho abbastanza.'	'Have you got enough money?' 'Yes, I have enough (of it).'
Se c'è ancora del te, *ne* prendo un'altra tazza.	If there's still some tea, I'll have another cup (of it).
Se compri le mele, *ne* prendi un chilo anche per me?	If you're buying apples, will you get a kilo (of them) for me as well?
'Volete ancora del cioccolato?' 'No, grazie, non *ne* vogliamo più.'	'Do you want some more chocolate?' 'No, thanks, we don't want any more (of it).'

Note, however, that **ne** is not used in cases where English would say 'all of it', 'all of them', etc. Compare the following examples:

'Quanti panini vuoi?' 'Ne voglio uno.'
'How many sandwiches do you want?' 'I want one (of them).'

'Quanti panini vuoi?' 'Li voglio tutti.'
'How many sandwiches do you want?' 'I want them all/all of them.'

'Quante arance hai mangiato?' 'Ne ho mangiate due.'
'How many oranges did you eat?' 'I ate two (of them).'

'Quante arance hai mangiato?' 'Le ho mangiate tutte.'
'How many oranges did you eat?' 'I ate them all/all of them.'

2 The pronoun **ne** is invariable, and can thus replace any noun, whether masculine, feminine, singular or plural:

'Quanto zucchero [ms] **compri?**' '**Ne compro due chili.**'
'How much sugar are you buying?' 'I'm getting two kilos.'

'Quanta farina [fs] **compri?**' '**Ne compro solo mezzo chilo.**'
'How much flour are you going to get?' 'I'm only getting half a kilo.'

'Quanti amici [mp] **inviti?**' '**Ne invito tre.**'
'How many friends are you inviting?' 'I'm inviting three.'

'Quante mele [fp] **vuoi?**' '**Ne voglio tre chili.**'
'How many apples do you want?' 'I want three kilos.'

3 As we have seen, **ne** is used when referring to partial quantities, however expressed. Some expressions which require the use of **ne** are the adverb **abbastanza** (enough/quite), the adjectives **molto, poco, troppo, alcuni/alcune** (some/any (plural)), and the pronoun **qualcuno/qualcuna** (some/any), which is always *singular*:

Non ho comprato del pane perché ne ho ancora abbastanza.
I didn't buy any bread because I've still got enough.

'**Hai molti CD?**' '**Sì, ne ho molti.**'
'Have you got many CDs?' 'Yes, I've got a lot.'

'**Hai tutti i libri che ti servono?**' '**No, ne ho solo alcuni.**'
'Have you got all the books you need?' 'No, I've only got a few.'

Quei biscotti sono molto buoni, ne prendo ancora qualcuno.
Those biscuits are very good, I'll have some more.

4 **Ne** is also used in negative expressions such as **non ... affatto** (not ... at all), **non ... nessuno/nessuna** (not ... anyone), **non ... più** (not ... any more):

'**Bevi molto caffè?**' '**No, non ne bevo affatto.**'
'Do you drink much coffee?' 'No, I don't drink it at all.'

Ho invitato dieci amici, ma non ne è venuto nessuno.
I invited ten friends, but none of them came.

'Hai ancora soldi?' 'No, non ne ho   'Have you still got money?' 'No, I've
   più.'   got none left.'

As these examples show, the negative is formed by putting **non** before **ne**.

Agreement of the past participle

When **ne** is used with a verb in the present perfect (or any other compound tense), there are certain rules governing the agreement of the past participle.

5 When **ne** is used in a sentence where the quantity is expressed by a number, the past participle must agree in gender with the noun it replaces, and in number (i.e. singular or plural) with the quantity of what **ne** stands for. Take this question:

Quante riviste hai comprato?   How many magazines did you buy?

In the answer to this question, the ending of **comprato** will depend on the *gender* of **rivista** (feminine) and on whether you bought *one* magazine (singular) or *more than* one (plural):

   Ne ho comprat*a* una [fs].   I bought one.
   Ne ho comprat*e* due [fp].   I bought two.

The same applies when **ne** replaces a masculine noun:

   Quanti esercizi [m] avete fatto?   How many exercises have
                                             you done?

Here, the ending of **fatto** must be masculine, but whether it is singular or plural will depend on how many exercises have been done:

   Ne abbiamo fatt*o* uno solo [ms].   We've only done one.
   Ne abbiamo fatt*i* quattro [mp].   We've done four.

The same rule applies when the quantity is expressed by **qualcuno/qualcuna** (remember that this is always singular) or **alcuni/alcune** (plural):

   **Dovevo fare molti *esercizi*, ma ne
      ho fatto solo *qualcuno*.**
   **Dovevo fare molti *esercizi*, ma ne
      ho fatti solo *alcuni*.**
                                             I was supposed to do a lot of exercises,
                                                but I only did a few.

'Quante *riviste* hai comprato?' 'Ne
  ho comprat*a qualcuna*.'
'Quante *riviste* hai comprato?' 'Ne
  ho comprat*e alcune*.'

> 'How many magazines did you buy?'
> 'I bought a few.'

6 When the quantity is expressed by an adverb or an adjective, the past participle agrees with the noun replaced by **ne**:

'**Hai comprato abbastanza** *pane* [ms]?' '**Sì, ne ho comprat***o abbastanza*.'	'Have you bought enough bread?' 'Yes, I've bought enough.'
'**Hai comprato abbastanza** *patatine* [fp]?' '**Sì, ne ho comprat***e abbastanza*.'	'Have you bought enough crisps?' 'Yes, I've bought enough.'
'**Quanta** *pasta* [fs] **avete mangiato?**' '**Ne abbiamo mangiat***a molta*.'	'How much pasta did you eat?' 'We ate a lot.'
'**Quante** *persone* [fp] **hai invitato?**' '**Ne ho invitat***e poche*.'	'How many people did you invite?' 'I only invited a few.'
'**Quanti** *esercizi* [mp] **hai fatto?**' '**Ne ho fatt***i alcuni*.'	'How many exercises did you do?' 'I did a few.'

7 When the quantity is expressed by a noun, the past participle can agree *either* with the quantity (this is more usual) *or* with the noun replaced by **ne**:

'**Quanto caffè hai bevuto?**' '**Ne ho**
  bevut*a una tazza* [fs].'
'**Quanto** *caffè* [ms] **hai bevuto?**' '**Ne**
  ho bevut*o una tazza*.'

> 'How much coffee did you drink?'
> 'I drank a cup.'

'**Quanto pane hai mangiato?**' '**Ne ho**
  mangiat*a una fetta* [fs].'
'**Quanto** *pane* [ms] **hai mangiato?**'
  '**Ne ho mangiat***o una fetta*.'

> 'How much bread did you eat?'
> 'I ate a slice.'

'**Quante caramelle hai mangiato?**' '**Ne**
  ho mangiat*o un pacchetto* [ms].'
'**Quante** *caramelle* [fp] **hai mangiato?**'
  '**Ne ho mangiat***e un pacchetto*.'

> 'How many sweets did you eat?'
> 'I ate a packet.'

'**Quanti biscotti hai mangiato?**' '**Ne ho**
  mangiat*a una scatola* [fs].'
'**Quanti** *biscotti* [mp] **hai mangiato?**'
  '**Ne ho mangiat***i una scatola*.'

> 'How many biscuits did you eat?'
> 'I ate a box.'

8 When **ne** occurs in a sentence together with a verb in the infinitive (usually after **dovere**, **potere**, **volere** or **sapere**), it can be attached to the infinitive. In such cases, when the main verb is in the present perfect (or any other compound tense) the past participle does not agree:

'Quanti libri hai letto?' 'Ho dovuto leggerne tre.'

'How many books did you read?' 'I had to read three.'

C'erano molti esercizi, ma ho potuto farne solo alcuni.

There were a lot of exercises, but I could only do a few.

Il compito era difficile e ho saputo farne solo una parte.

The homework was difficult, and I could only do part of it.

However, if **ne** is not attached to the infinitive, the past participle must agree, in the same way as in the rules given in paragraphs 5–7:

'Quanti libri hai letto?' 'Ne ho dovut*i* leggere tre.'

'How many books did you read?' 'I had to read three.'

C'erano molti esercizi, ma ne ho potut*i* fare solo alcuni.

There were a lot of exercises, but I could only do a few.

Gli esercizi erano difficili e ne ho saput*a* fare solo una parte [fs].

Gli esercizi [mp] erano difficili e ne ho saput*i* fare solo una parte.

The exercises were difficult, and I could only do part of them.

9 Another use of **ne** is is to replace a noun (or a pronoun) preceded by the preposition **di** (as in **Parliamo *del* libro di Primo Levi**, 'We're talking about Primo Levi's book'):

Conosco questo film: ieri *ne* parlavano alla radio.

I know this film: they were talking about it on the radio yesterday.

È un libro di successo: tutti *ne* parlano.

It's a popular book: everybody's talking about it.

Hai visto lo spettacolo? Che *ne* pensi?

Did you see the show? What do you think of it?

Ha molti problemi, ma non *ne* parla mai.

He has a lot of problems, but he never talks about them.

When **ne** is used in this way, the past participle does not agreee:

Marco aveva dei problemi e ne ha parlato con Anna.

Marco had problems, and talked about them with Anna.

Questi sono libri di successo e tutti ne hanno parlato.

These are popular books and everybody's been talking about them.

The pronoun *ci*

10 The pronoun **ci** is used to replace a noun denoting a place; it corresponds to the English 'there'. We have already seen this pronoun used with the verb **essere** in expressions like **c'è** and **ci sono** (Unit 4), but it can be used with other verbs, always preceding them:

'Quando vai in biblioteca?' '*Ci* vado oggi pomeriggio.'	'When are you going to the library?' 'I'm going (there) this afternoon.'
Conosco bene Bologna: *ci* ho passato due anni.	I know Bologna well: I spent two years there.
'Ogni quanto va in palestra?' 'Non *ci* vado mai.'	'How often do you go to the gym?' 'I never go (there).'

As the examples suggest, **ci** is used more often in this kind of sentence than 'there' is in English.

11 **Ci** always comes before the verb. Like the other unstressed pronouns, though, it can be attached to the infinitive of a verb (usually after **dovere**, **potere**, **volere** or **sapere**):

Dovevo andare a Fiesole, ma non sapevo andarci. **Dovevo andare a Fiesole, ma non ci sapevo andare.**	I had to go to Fiesole, but I didn't know how to get there.
Vado al mercato, vuoi venirci anche tu? **Vado al mercato, ci vuoi venire anche tu?**	I'm going to the market, would you like to come (as well)?

Exercise 1

Supply the pronoun **ne**, making sure that the past participle and the adjective or pronoun agree where necessary.

Examples: 'Quante lettere hai scritto?' '____ ho scritt____ alcun____.': <u>Ne</u> ho scritt<u>e</u> alcune; Mi piacciono i biscotti e ____ ho mangiat____ molt____: <u>ne</u> ho mangiat<u>i</u> molti; 'Quanti libri hai letto?' 'Non ____ ho lett____ nessun____.': Non <u>ne</u> ho lett<u>o</u> nessun<u>o</u>.

1 'Quante cartoline hai mandato?' '____ ho mandat____ 12.'
2 'Hai comprato i biscotti?' ' Sì, ____ ho comprat____ una scatola.'

3 'Hai fatto i compiti?' '____ ho fatt____ la metà.'
4 'Quante persone sono venute?' '____ sono venut____ poch____.'
5 'Quanti errori hai fatto?' 'Non ____ ho fatt____ nessun____.'
6 'Hai chiuso tutte le finestre?' 'No, ____ ho lasciat____ una apert____.'
7 'Quanti amici hanno invitato?' '____ hanno invitat____ molt____.'
8 'Quanti libri hai letto?' '____ ho lett____ due.'
9 'Quanta pasta avete comprato?' '____ abbiamo comprat____ poc____.'
10 'Quante caramelle hai mangiato?' 'Non ____ ho mangiat____ nessun____.'
11 'Quanti francobolli hai preso?' '____ ho pres____ abbastanza.'
12 Avevo molte riviste e ____ ho dat____ alcun____ a Luigi.
13 Ci piacciono i film comici e ieri sera ____ abbiamo vist____ tre.
14 Ho fatto una torta e ____ ho mangiat____ due fette.
15 La zia ha portato dei cioccolatini ma Piero non ____ ha mangiat____ nessun____.
16 Abbiamo molti videogiochi e ____ abbiamo dat____ qualcun____ a Michele.
17 C'erano molti libri interessanti e ____ ho pres____ alcun____.
18 Hanno venduto molti CD e ____ sono rimast____ solo alcun____ molto car____.
19 C'erano molte ragazze, ma Marco non ____ ha invitat____ nessun____.
20 Ho comprato tre magliette e ____ ho regalat____ due a mio fratello.

Exercise 2

Complete with the appropriate pronouns: direct object or **ne**.

Examples: 'Quanti amici hai?' '____ ho molti.': ne; 'Quanti amici inviti?' '____ invito tutti.': li

1 'Hai fatto tutti gli esercizi?' 'No, non ____ ho fatto nessuno.'
2 'Quante sorelle hai?' '____ ho due.'
3 Avevo molti CD dei Beatles, ma ____ ho imprestati tutti.
4 'Hai fatto il compito?' 'No, non ____ho ancora fatto.'
5 'Vuoi del dolce?' 'No grazie, non ____ voglio.'
6 Stamattina ho comprato due riviste e ____ ho lette nel pomeriggio.
7 'Hai fatto molti sbagli?' '____ ho fatto uno solo.'
8 Il dolce era molto buono e ____ ho mangiate tre fette.
9 Mi piacciono i film di Fellini e ____ ho visti tutti.
10 Ho comprato tre libri, ma non ____ ho letto nessuno.
11 Avevo due biglietti da 10 euro, ma ____ ho perso uno.
12 Ieri ho preso lo stipendio, ma ____ho già speso tutto.
13 Se ci sono ancora dei biscotti, ____ prendo due o tre.

14 Era un argomento interessante e ____ abbiamo parlato molto.
15 Il film era noioso e ____ abbiamo visto solo metà.
16 Carla parte: ____ accompagno alla stazione.
17 Lo zucchero è finito: ____ compri tu?
18 'Vuoi dello zucchero nel caffè?' 'Sì, ____ voglio due cucchiaini.'
19 Ho comprato tre brioches e ____ ho mangiate due.
20 'Conoscete tutti i componenti del gruppo?' 'Sì, ____ conosciamo tutti.'

Exercise 3

Rewrite the sentences as in the example.

Example: Ne vuoi prendere ancora?: Vuoi prenderne ancora?

1 Ne dovete parlare col professore.
2 Ne vuoi fare un altro?
3 Non ne dobbiamo prendere.
4 Ne potete mangiare.
5 Ne devo fare sei.
6 Non ne possiamo parlare.
7 Ne posso assaggiare uno?
8 Non ne deve portare, Signora.
9 Ne vogliono comprare qualcuno.
10 Non ne possono bere.

Exercise 4

Rewrite the sentences as in the example. Make sure that the past participle agrees where necessary.

Example: Ha voluto portarne un po' [fs]: Ne ha voluta portare un po'.

1 Ho dovuto darne due [m] a Marisa.
2 Hai potuto comprarne [fp]?
3 Quante hai dovuto farne?
4 Non hanno voluto mangiarne [fs].
5 Ha dovuto leggerne quattro [mp].
6 Non abbiamo potuto prenderne [fp].
7 Ho dovuto scriverne due [fp].
8 Ho potuto leggerne solo due pagine.
9 Avete dovuto rifarne molti?
10 Non hanno potuto assaggiarne [fs].

Exercise 5

Identify the words that can be replaced by the pronoun **ci**, and rewrite the sentences with **ci** in the right place.

   Example: Vai a Roma in aereo?: a Roma; Ci vai in aereo?

 1 Abitiamo in questa casa da tre anni.
 2 Stefano lavora al Museo di Storia Naturale da febbraio.
 3 Volete venire alla festa di Marco?
 4 Paola e Livia vanno al cinema due volte alla settimana.
 5 La Signora Bini va sempre al supermercato a piedi.
 6 Rimango in Italia per tre settimane.
 7 Giulia viene sempre a scuola in bici.
 8 Ho passato tre ore in coda all'ufficio postale.
 9 Siete andati a cena a casa di Pietro?
10 Passiamo le vacanze a Sorrento.

UNIT EIGHTEEN
The future tense

Use of the future

1 The future tense is, of course, used to refer to events which will happen in the future, as in the following examples:

Venerdì *andremo* in piscina.	On Friday we'll go to the swimming pool.
Non so quando *partirò*.	I don't know when I'll leave.
Verrà anche l'anno prossimo, Signora?	Will you come/be coming again next year(, Madam?)

2 The future is also used to express probability, or a guess:

Anna non risponde: *sarà* fuori.	Anna's not answering: she must/she'll be out.
***Saranno* le 5.**	It's probably/It'll be about 5 o'clock.
La madre di Pietro *avrà* 30 anni.	Pietro's mother must be around 30.
Chi *sarà*?	Who can that be?

3 The future can also correspond to the English present progressive ('I'm going to . . .' etc.):

Gli *parlerò* presto.	I'm going to talk/I'll be talking to them soon.
***Porterò* i miei CD.**	I'm going to bring/I'll be bringing my CDs.
Gli *direte* la verità?	Are you going to tell him the truth?

4 In general, the future tense is used less in Italian than in English, and it is often possible, when talking about something which we are almost sure will happen, to use the present:

Partono domani.	They'll leave/They're leaving tomorrow.
Viene anche l'anno prossimo, Signora?	Will you come/be coming again next year(, Madam?)
L'anno prossimo sono all'università.	Next year I'll be at university.

5 However, in certain cases Italian uses the future where English uses the present. Take this English sentence: 'When/If I earn/am earning good money, I'll buy a car.' Here, 'when' and 'if' actually refer to an action *in the future*; in cases like this, Italian normally uses the future tense:

Se guadagnerò bene, comprerò una macchina.	If I earn/am earning good money, I'll buy a car.
Quando arriverà, le mostreremo il centro commerciale.	When she arrives, we'll show her the shopping mall.

The forms of the future indicative

6 The future endings for the three conjugations are as follows:

	-are	*-ere*	*-ire*
(io)	**-erò**	**-erò**	**-irò**
(tu)	**-erai**	**-erai**	**-irai**
(lui/lei)	**-erà**	**-erà**	**-irà**
(noi)	**-eremo**	**-eremo**	**-iremo**
(voi)	**-erete**	**-erete**	**-irete**
(loro)	**-eranno**	**-eranno**	**-iranno**

Regular verbs ending in **-are** are conjugated as follows:

Parlare	*To speak*
parlerò	I will speak
parlerai	you will speak
parlerà	he/she/it will speak
parleremo	we will speak
parlerete	you will speak
parleranno	they will speak

Regular verbs ending in **-ere** are conjugated as follows:

Prendere	*To take*/get
pren**derò**	I will take/get
pren**derai**	you will take/get
pren**derà**	he/she/it will take/get
pren**deremo**	we will take/get
pren**derete**	you will take/get
pren**deranno**	they will take/get

Regular verbs ending in **-ire** are conjugated as follows:

Partire	*To leave*
part**irò**	I will leave
part**irai**	you will leave
part**irà**	he/she/it will leave
part**iremo**	we will leave
part**irete**	you will leave
part**iranno**	they will leave

Dopo un mese in Italia, *parlerai* **meglio italiano.**	After a month in Italy, you'll speak Italian better.
Prenderò **il treno delle 8.**	I'll get the eight o'clock train.
Partiranno **domani mattina presto.**	They will leave early tomorrow morning.
Domenica prossima *finirò* **di lavorare verso le 5.**	Next Sunday I'll finish work at about five.

7 Verbs ending in **-care** and **-gare** add **h** before the endings of the future in order to keep the hard sound of **c** and **g**:

Cercare	*Pagare*
cer**cherò**	pa**gherò**
cer**cherai**	pa**gherai**
cer**cherà**	pa**gherà**
cer**cheremo**	pa**gheremo**
cer**cherete**	pa**gherete**
cer**cheranno**	pa**gheranno**

Quando arriveremo a Roma *cercheremo* **un albergo economico.**	When we arrive in Rome we'll look for a cheap hotel.
Mio padre *pagherà* **tutte le spese.**	My father will pay all the expenses.

8 Verbs ending in **-ciare** and **-giare** drop **-i** in the future:

Cominciare	*Mangiare*
comincerò	mangerò
comincerai	mangerai
comincerà	mangerà
cominceremo	mangeremo
comincerete	mangerete
cominceranno	mangeranno

Comincerò a lavorare venerdì prossimo. — I'll start work(ing) next Friday.

Mangerai in mensa? — Will you eat/be eating in the canteen?

Future of some irregular verbs

9 **Essere** and **avere** are irregular:

Essere	*Avere*
sarò	avrò
sarai	avrai
sarà	avrà
saremo	avremo
sarete	avrete
saranno	avranno

Se domenica *sarà* bello lavoreremo in giardino. — If the weather is good on Sunday, we'll work in the garden.

Se *avrò* tempo ti aiuterò. — If I've got time, I'll help you.

10 **Dare**, **fare** and **stare** follow the same pattern as **essere**:

Dare	*Fare*	*Stare*
darò	farò	starò
darai	farai	starai
darà	farà	starà
daremo	faremo	staremo
darete	farete	starete
daranno	faranno	staranno

Mia sorella *darà* una festa per il suo compleanno.	My sister will give/is giving a party for her birthday.
Cosa *farai* dopo l'università?	What will you do/are you doing after university?
Domani *starai* meglio.	You'll feel better tomorrow.

11 **Andare**, **cadere** (to fall), **dovere**, **potere**, **sapere**, **vedere** and **vivere** follow the same pattern as **avere**:

Andare	*Cadere*	*Dovere*	*Potere*
andrò	cadrò	dovrò	potrò
andrai	cadrai	dovrai	potrai
andrà	cadrà	dovrà	potrà
andremo	cadremo	dovremo	potremo
andrete	cadrete	dovrete	potrete
andranno	cadranno	dovranno	potranno

Sapere	*Vedere*	*Vivere*
saprò	vedrò	vivrò
saprai	vedrai	vivrai
saprà	vedrà	vivrà
sapremo	vedremo	vivremo
saprete	vedrete	vivrete
sapranno	vedranno	vivranno

Andremo alla festa solo se ci inviteranno.	We'll only go to the party if they invite us.
Il governo è impopolare e *cadrà* presto.	The government is unpopular and will soon fall.
Credo che *dovrò* partire presto.	I think I'll have to leave early.
Non so se *potrò* venire.	I don't know whether I'll be able to come.
Non *sapremo* mai la verità.	We will never know the truth.
Quando *vedrai* i tuoi amici?	When will you/are you going to see your friends?

12 A third group of irregular verbs, comprising **bere**, **rimanere**, **venire**, **volere** and **tenere** (to keep/hold), have the following pattern:

	Bere	*Rimanere*	*Venire*	*Volere*	*Tenere*
-rrò	berrò	rimarrò	verrò	vorrò	terrò
-rrai	berrai	rimarrai	verrai	vorrai	terrai
-rrà	berrà	rimarrà	verrà	vorrà	terrà
-rremo	berremo	rimarremo	verremo	vorremo	terremo
-rrete	berrete	rimarrete	verrete	vorrete	terrete
-rranno	berranno	rimarranno	verranno	vorranno	terranno

Sono sicuro che mio fratello non
   ***berrà* mai quella tisana.**
I'm sure my brother will never drink
   that herbal tea.

Quanto tempo *rimarrete* in Italia,
   Signori Boi?
How long will you/are you going to
   stay in Italy, Mrs and Mr Boi?

Hanno detto che *verranno* a trovarci. They said they'll come and see us.

Non so se *vorrò* andare
   all'università, dopo il liceo.
I don't know whether I'll want to go
   to university after secondary
   school.

Dove *terrai* la bici?
Where are you going to keep the bike?

13 All verbs ending in **-urre** have the following pattern:

	Tradurre
-urrò	tradurrò
-urrai	tradurrai
-urrà	tradurrà
-urremo	tradurremo
-urrete	tradurrete
-urranno	tradurranno

Carlo non parla tedesco, ma un
   interprete *tradurrà* tutto per lui.
Carlo doesn't speak German, but an
   interpreter is going to/will translate
   everything for him.

Negative form

14 As usual, the negative is formed by putting **non** before the verb:

Non andrò alla festa.   I'm not going to the party.
Non rimarremo molto.   We won't stay long.
Non gli parlerò mai più!   I'll never speak to him again!

Exercise 1

Supply the future tense of the verb in brackets.

Example: Non (io partire) tanto presto: partirò

1 I miei amici (arrivare) domani.
2 Quando (voi parlare) con Maria?
3 (lui telefonare) domani.
4 Gli (tu dire) tutto?
5 Domani (io scrivere) ai nonni.
6 Domenica (io dormire) fino a tardi.
7 (noi cominciare) a lavorare domani.
8 Quando (tu finire) il compito?
9 Stasera (io prendere) l'auto.
10 Mi (tu chiamare)?
11 Dove (voi abitare)?
12 (loro portare) il dolce.
13 Cosa le (voi dire)?
14 Chi (tradurre) dal tedesco?
15 Domani (noi pagare) l'affitto.
16 (tu mangiare) con noi?
17 Mi (Lei scrivere), Signora?
18 Paul (cercare) casa a Torino.
19 Che treno (loro prendere)?
20 Chi (pagare)?

Exercise 2

Supply the future tense of the verb in brackets.

Example: Non (io dovere) andare a scuola: dovrò

1 (io andare) in vacanza.
2 (noi essere) contenti di vedervi.
3 Quanto tempo (tu rimanere) a Roma?
4 (io venire) appena (io potere).
5 (Lei dovere) partire, Signora?
6 (lei venire) quando (lei volere).
7 Domani non (noi avere) tempo.
8 Non so se (io potere) uscire.
9 Quando (tu vedere) Anna?
10 (voi fare) una festa?
11 Non (loro stare) a casa mia.
12 Non lo (lui sapere) mai.
13 Gli (tu fare) un regalo?
14 (voi essere) a casa tutto il giorno?
15 (voi dovere) lavorare domani?
16 Non (io andare) più in quel bar.
17 Quando (tu sapere) il risultato?
18 Quando (tu venire), Maria?
19 Cosa (voi fare) domenica?
20 (loro tenere) il cane in giardino.

Exercise 3

Change the verbs in *italics* into the future.

Domani mattina *esco* di casa presto: *devo* prendere il treno per Firenze alle
6.15. *Arrivo* a Firenze verso ora di pranzo e Lorenzo *viene* a prendermi alla

stazione. Prima *andiamo* a casa sua dove *lascio* i bagagli e poi *andiamo* insieme a pranzo da Ernestina. Nel pomeriggio *vediamo* Carlo che ci *porta* a vedere la sua nuova casa. *Torniamo* a casa di Lorenzo abbastanza presto perché *vengono* degli amici a cena e *dobbiamo* preparare. Dopo cena *usciamo*, ma, anche se *facciamo* tardi, non *è* un problema perché *possiamo* dormire la mattina dopo.

Exercise 4

Translate into Italian:

1 Who will be able to help me?
2 Next summer we'll do an Italian course.
3 Will you [sing.] read all these books?
4 I won't go to the library tomorrow.
5 When will you arrive, Signora Pasini?
6 On Sunday, they'll go out.
7 What will you [sing.] do?
8 It'll be about ten o'clock.
9 Will you [sing.] bring your CDs for the party?
10 Won't you [pl.] come to the cinema with us?

UNIT NINETEEN
The past perfect tense

Use of the past perfect

1 The past perfect (or pluperfect) normally indicates a past event which happened before another past event, as in the English 'I *had finished* showering when I heard the doorbell', 'By the time it finished, I *had had* enough.' It is thus normally used in sentences where there is another past tense, or some other reference to a past event:

Quando sono arrivato [present perfect] *avevano* **appena** *finito* [past perfect] **di cenare.**	When I arrived they had just finished dinner.
Quel giorno *ero* [imperfect] **molto contenta perché** *avevo passato* [past perfect] **l'esame.**	That day I was very happy because I'd passed the exam.
Prima di imprestare [infinitive] **l'auto a Marco,** *avevo fatto* [past perfect] **il pieno.**	Before lending the car to Marco, I'd filled up.

It is also often used on its own, where a more recent event is referred to, or implied, in the context:

Avevo fatto quella torta per te, non per Paolo.	I made that tart for you, not for Paolo. [e.g. that's why I'm so annoyed that Paolo's eaten it]
Tullio aveva portato i CD.	Tullio had brought the CDs. [e.g. the ones I told you we were listening to]
Francesca era uscita.	Francesca had gone out. [e.g. which is why I didn't see her last night]

2 Sometimes, when the past perfect is used on its own, the event nearer to the present is purely implicit:

Scusa, non ti avevo visto! È molto che aspetti?	Sorry, I didn't see you. Have you been waiting long?

Implied here is something like **(Ora ti ho visto, ma prima) non ti avevo visto** [i.e. I've seen you now, but I hadn't before].

Scusa, non ti *avevo sentito*.	Sorry, I didn't hear you.

Implied here is something like **Non ti avevo sentito (ma ora ti ho sentito)** [i.e. I hadn't heard you before, but I have now].

Forming the past perfect

3 The past perfect in Italian is formed with the imperfect indicative of **avere** or **essere** (auxiliary verbs) followed by the past participle of the verb. Here are two examples, one using **avere** and the other **essere**:

Imperfect of avere	*Past participle of scrivere*	
(io) **avevo**	**scritto**	I had written
(tu) **avevi**	**scritto**	you had written
(lui/lei) **aveva**	**scritto**	he/she/it had written
(noi) **avevamo**	**scritto**	we had written
(voi) **avevate**	**scritto**	you had written
(loro) **avevano**	**scritto**	they had written

Imperfect of essere	*Past participle of andare*	
(io) **ero**	**andato/andata**	I had gone
(tu) **eri**	**andato/andata**	you had gone
(lui/lei) **era**	**andato/andata**	he/she/it had gone
(noi) **eravamo**	**andati/andate**	we had gone
(voi) **eravate**	**andati/andate**	you had gone
(loro) **erano**	**andati/andate**	they had gone

4 As regards agreement of the past participle, the past perfect obeys exactly the same rules as the present perfect: if the auxiliary is **avere** the past participle does not change; but if it is **essere** the past participle behaves like an adjective, agreeing in gender and number with the subject of the verb, as in these examples:

Avere

Livia aveva guardato la televisione.	Livia had watched television.
Avevi comprato il pane?	Had you bought the bread?
Aveva prenotato, Signor Ferro?	Had you booked, Mr Ferro?

Essere

Monica era uscit*a*. [fs]

Pietro era stat*o* malato. [ms]   Monica had gone out.

Fabia e Silvia erano rimast*e* a casa. Pietro had been ill.
  [fp]   Fabia and Silvia had stayed at home.

Giulia e Sebastiano erano partit*i*.
  [mp]   Giulia and Sebastiano had left.

Ero andat*a* al cinema. [fs]

       I had been/gone to the cinema. [the
Eravamo arrivat*i* tardi. [mp]   speaker is female]
       We had arrived late. [the speakers are
Signor Poli, Lei quando era   males or a mixed group]
  arrivat*o*?* [ms]   When had you arrived, Mr Poli?
Signora Poli, Lei quando era
  arrivat*a*?* [fs]   When had you arrived, Mrs Poli?

* When the polite form is used and the auxiliary is **essere**, the past participle agrees with the gender of the person being spoken to, not with **Lei**.

Past perfect of *avere* and *essere*

5 **Avere** forms the past perfect with the auxiliary **avere**:

avevo avuto	I had had
avevi avuto	you had had
aveva avuto	he/she/it had had
avevamo avuto	we had had
avevate avuto	you had had
avevano avuto	they had had

Essere forms the past perfect with the auxiliary **essere**:

ero stato/stata	I had been
eri stato/stata	you had been
era stato/stata	he/she/it had been
eravamo stati/state	we had been
eravate stati/state	you had been
erano stati/state	they had been

Non aveva avuto tempo di finire il   He hadn't had time to finish the job.
  lavoro.
Tanya aveva avuto la varicella.   Tanya had had chickenpox.

Nina era stata malata.	Nina had been ill.
Des era stato mio studente.	Des had been a student of mine.

Negative form

6 The negative is formed in the same way as for the present perfect, by placing **non** before the verb:

Non ero andato a scuola.	I hadn't been/gone to school.
Lisa non era riuscita a finire quel lavoro.	Lisa hadn't managed to finish that job.
Non avevi telefonato la settimana prima?	Had you not phoned the previous week?

7 As with the present perfect, the adverbs **mai** (ever), **più** (more/again) and **già** (already) are normally placed between the auxiliary and the verb (e.g. **Avevo** *già* **risposto**, 'I'd already replied'). With the negatives **non . . . ancora** (not . . . yet), **non . . . mai** (never), **non . . . più** (not . . . any more/not . . . again/no . . . longer), **non** is placed before the auxiliary:

Eravate *mai* **stati su un ghiacciaio?**	Had you ever been on a glacier?
Avevi *più* **visto i tuoi amici?**	Had you (ever) seen your friends again?
***Non* avevamo *ancora* preso il biglietto.**	We hadn't bought the ticket yet.
Paola *non* era *mai* stata a Venezia.	Paola had never been to Venice.
Carlo *non* aveva *più* telefonato.	Carlo hadn't (ever) phoned again.

Exercise 1

Supply the past perfect of the verb in brackets.

Example: Dove (tu comprare) quelle scarpe?: avevi comprato

1 Maria (finire) di cenare.
2 Anna (arrivare) il giorno prima.
3 Scusi, Signora, non La (io vedere)!
4 (tu spegnere) la luce?
5 (voi prendere) il giornale?
6 Prima di lavorare in Italia, Jim (lavorare) in Francia.
7 Hai perso la lettera che ti (scrivere) Antonio?
8 Alessandro non (preparare) l'esame.
9 Non (tu riuscire) a finire il lavoro?
10 Gli (noi chiedere) dei CD.
11 Caterina (stare) male.

12 (io mangiare) un panino, ma
    avevo ancora fame.
13 Ti (piacere) la partita?
14 Cecilia (andare) in vacanza.
15 Le mie amiche (uscire).
16 Non (io capire) nulla.

17 Il treno (partire) in orario.
18 Sergio (rimanere) in ufficio.
19 Paolo non (volere) lavorare con
    noi.
20 Gina (essere) contenta di vedermi.

Exercise 2

Complete the following sentences, using the correct tense of the verb in brackets (present perfect, imperfect or past perfect).

    Example: Carlo (raccontare) che (lui passare) l'esame, ma non (essere) vero: Carlo ha raccontato che aveva passato l'esame, ma non era vero.

1 Quando (io arrivare) i miei amici (uscire) da poco.
2 Silvia non (conoscere) la persona che le (telefonare).
3 (tu fare) un dolce? Ma ti (io dire) che sono a dieta!
4 Ernestina (essere) stanca perché (camminare) molto.
5 Carlo non (venire) con noi perché (dovere) fare un lavoro che gli (loro dare) la sera prima.
6 Silvio (essere) molto contento perché (vincere) la gara di sci.
7 Carla (portare) sempre la maglia che le (regalare) suo fratello.
8 (io comprare) i libri che mi (voi consigliare).
9 Mauro (spendere) tutti i soldi che (lui guadagnare).
10 Francesca (invitare) tutti gli amici che (andare) in vacanza con lei l'anno prima.

Exercise 3

Translate into Italian:

1 Paola still hadn't been to Scotland.
2 I'd finished the job, but I was very tired.
3 The girls had never gone into that church.
4 Arianna finished the tart her grandmother had made.
5 'What had you [sing.] said to Fabio?' 'I hadn't said anything to him.'
6 Maria had had to stay at home.
7 How much had your [pl.] car cost?

8 They'd bought the ticket the previous day.
9 I hadn't got the bike any longer, because I'd given it to Anna.
10 She was born in Russia, but she'd been living in Italy for many years when I met her.

UNIT TWENTY
Reflexive pronouns

1 Reflexive pronouns correspond to 'myself', 'yourself', etc. in phrases like 'you flatter yourself', 'the cat's licking itself', 'the recorder's switched itself off'. In such cases, the subject and the object of the verb are the same person or thing:

Ti **guardi sempre allo specchio.**	You always look at yourself in the mirror.
Mi **lavo.**	I get washed. [lit. I wash myself]
Anna *si* **veste per la festa.**	Anna's getting dressed for the party. [lit. Anna's dressing herself]

These examples show how the reflexive pronouns are the direct objects of the verbs **lavare**, **guardare** and **vestire** and denote the same person as the subject.

There are very many verbs which can be used in the reflexive form in Italian and which do not correspond to English reflexive verbs. Here is a list of some of the most common ones:

addormentarsi	to fall asleep [lit. to send oneself to sleep]
alzarsi	to get up [lit. to raise oneself]
annoiarsi	to get/be bored [lit. to bore oneself]
dimenticarsi	to forget [lit. to forget oneself]
lavarsi	to get washed [lit. to wash oneself]
offendersi	to take offence [lit. to offend oneself]
ricordarsi	to remember [lit. to recall oneself]
riposarsi	to rest [lit. to rest oneself]
sbagliarsi	to be wrong/mistaken [lit. to mistake oneself]
scusarsi	to apologise [lit. to excuse oneself]
sedersi	to sit down [lit. to seat oneself]
sentirsi	to feel (well, ill, etc.) [lit. to feel oneself]
svegliarsi	to wake up [lit. to waken oneself]
vestirsi	to get dressed [lit. to dress oneself]

2 The forms of the reflexive pronouns are as follows:

mi	myself
ti	yourself
si	himself/herself/itself
ci	ourselves
vi	yourselves
si	themselves

A che ora ti alzi, la mattina?	What time do you get up in the morning?
Paolo si* sveglia sempre tardi.	Paolo always wakes up late.
Maria si* annoia.	Maria is bored.
I tuoi amici si* sbagliano: il concerto non è stasera.	Your friends are wrong: the concert is not tonight.
Le mie amiche si* divertono.	My friends are enjoying themselves.

* Note that the third person singular and plural pronoun **si** is the same for masculine and feminine.

As can be seen from the examples, reflexive pronouns are always placed before the verb.

3 The negative is formed, as usual, by placing **non** before the pronoun:

Lorenzo non si annoia mai.	Lorenzo never gets/is never bored.
Non ti diverti?	Aren't you enjoying yourself?

4 For the formal form, the pronoun **si** (third person singular and plural) is used. In the plural, however, the pronoun **vi** is most frequently used:

Come si sente, Signora?	How are you feeling, Madam?
Vi divertite, Signori Rasi? } **(Si divertono, Signori Rasi?)** }	Are you enjoying yourselves(, Mr and Mrs Rasi)?

5 The plural forms of the reflexive pronouns (**ci**, **vi**, **si**) are also used as reciprocal pronouns, corresponding to the English 'each other':

Paolo e io non ci sopportiamo.	Paolo and I can't stand each other.
Perché vi guardate?	Why are you looking at each other?
Alfredo e Pia non si parlano più.	Alfredo and Pia don't talk to each other any more.

6 Reflexive pronouns can also be used, in contemporary spoken Italian, as indirect objects. One such use is to stress that the action expressed by the verb

is to the advantage of the subject (cf. English 'I'm making myself a coffee' [i.e. a coffee for myself], 'They're going to have themselves some fun' [i.e. some fun for themselves]):

Mi mangio un panino.	I'm going to eat a sandwich.
Perché non ci facciamo una partita a carte?	Why don't we have a game of cards?
Paolo si mangia sempre tutti i biscotti.	Paolo always eats all the biscuits.

7 Another common use of the Italian reflexive pronoun occurs in cases like the following, where English would use a possessive adjective ('my', 'your', etc.) rather than a reflexive pronoun:

Mi lavo le mani.	I wash my hands.
Ti metti il cappotto?	Are you going to put your coat on?
Anna si lava i capelli tutti i giorni.	Anna washes her hair every day.

8 When reflexive or reciprocal pronouns occur with a verb in the present perfect (or any other compound tense), the auxiliary is always **essere** (even if the verb itself would form the past tenses with **avere**), and the past participle always agrees with the subject:

Paolo si *è* svegliat*o* tardi.	Paolo woke up late.
Maria si *è* annoiat*a*.	Maria got bored.
Vittorio, a che ora *ti* sei alzat*o*?	Vittorio, what time did you get up?
Paolo e Francesca si *sono* sposat*i*.	Paolo and Francesca have got married.
Claudio e Anna si *sono* lavat*i* le mani.	Claudio and Anna washed their hands.
Sabina si *è* mangiat*a* un panino.	Sabina ate a sandwich.
Si *sono* fatt*i* un caffè.	They made (themselves) a coffee.

9 The reflexive pronouns, like all unstressed pronouns, can be attached to the infinitive of a verb (mainly after **dovere**, **potere**, **volere** or **sapere**). In these sentences, when the main verb is in the present perfect (or any other compound tense), the auxiliary is **avere**, and the past participle does *not* agree:

Devo alzarmi presto.	I've got to get up early.
Mio fratello non vuole lavarsi.	My brother doesn't want to wash.
Paolo e Francesca hanno voluto sposarsi.	Paolo and Francesca wanted to get married.
Non abbiamo potuto lavarci.	We couldn't wash.

However, when the reflexive pronoun is not attached to the infinitive, the auxiliary verb must be **essere**, and the past participle does agree:

**Paolo e Francesca si sono voluti
    sposare.**   Paolo and Francesca wanted to get
                                                     married.
Non ci siamo potuti lavare.   We couldn't wash.
Vi siete dovuti fermare per la notte?   Did you have to stop for the night?

Stressed forms

10 The reflexive pronouns also have stressed forms which are used, like the stressed forms of other pronouns, for emphasis and after a preposition. These forms are often reinforced by the adjective **stesso**:

me *or* **me stesso/stessa**   myself
te *or* **te stesso/stessa**   yourself
sé *or* **se* stesso/stessa**   himself/herself/itself
noi *or* **noi stessi/stesse**   ourselves
voi *or* **voi stessi/stesse**   yourselves
sé *or* **se* stessi/stesse**   themselves

Franca ama solo sé/se* stessa.   Franca only loves herself.
Pensi solo a te/te stesso!   You only think of yourself!
Quei due sono davvero noiosi: Those two are really boring: they only
    parlano solo di sè/se* stessi.   talk about themselves.

* Note that **se** does not have an accent when it is used with **stesso**.

Exercise 1

Insert the correct reflexive/reciprocal pronouns in the blank spaces.

   Example: A che ora _____ alzi?: <u>ti</u>

1 Quando _____ sposano?
2 Dove _____ siedo?
3 Nina non _____ veste mai di
   rosso.
4 Come _____ sentite?
5 Nina e Bart _____ amano.
6 Dove _____ incontriamo?
7 _____ lavo le mani.
8 Marina _____ guarda allo
   specchio.
9 Silvano non _____ annoia mai.
10 Carlo e Luca non _____
   conoscono.
11 Come _____ vestite?

12 Non _____ diverti?
13 _____ prendiamo un gelato?
14 Signora, _____ sente bene?
15 Non _____ ricordate di me?
16 Livia e Sara _____ riposano.

17 Paolo _____ sbaglia.
18 Come _____ chiami?
19 _____ scrivete spesso?
20 _____ offendono facilmente.

Exercise 2

Insert the correct reflexive/reciprocal pronouns in the blank spaces.

Example: A che ora _____ sono alzati?: si

1 Paolo _____ è offeso.
2 Anna _____ è arrabbiata.
3 Dove _____ siete conosciuti?
4 _____ sono alzati tardi.
5 Non _____ sei scusato con loro?
6 _____ siamo capiti subito.
7 Carla non _____ è messa il cappotto.
8 Il bambino _____ è addormentato.
9 Silvana e io _____ siamo viste ieri.
10 _____ sono mangiato un panino.
11 _____ siete vestiti molto bene.
12 Non _____ siamo capiti.
13 Daniela e Pino _____ odiano.
14 Quanta acqua _____ sei bevuto?
15 _____ sono tagliata un dito.
16 Perché _____ sei messo il golf?
17 _____ facciamo una passeggiata?
18 Sergio non _____ è ancora svegliato.
19 _____ sono sentita male.
20 _____ siete annoiati alla festa?

Exercise 3

Put the verbs into the present perfect:

Example: (tu [f] alzarsi) tardi: ti sei alzata

1 Antonio e Lia (sposarsi).
2 (tu [m] sbagliarsi)
3 (voi [f] ricordare) il suo compleanno?
4 Claudia (farsi) male.
5 (loro [m] incontrarsi) allo stadio.
6 (tu [m] perdersi)?
7 Signora, non (divertirsi)?
8 (noi [m] bersi) un litro di acqua.
9 Non (io [m] annoiarsi).
10 (noi [f] alzarsi) presto.
11 Non (tu [m] lavarsi) le mani?
12 (io [f] tagliarsi) i capelli.
13 Il treno (fermarsi).
14 I miei zii (separarsi).
15 Vittorio non (lamentarsi).
16 Il professore (riposarsi).
17 La professoressa (stancarsi).
18 Non (tu [f] arrabbiarsi)?
19 (voi [m] offendersi)?
20 (loro [m] dimenticarsi) di noi!

Exercise 4

Rewrite the sentences, moving the pronoun and changing the auxiliary.

   Example: Abbiamo dovuto alzarci [m]: Ci siamo dovuti alzare.

1   Non ho potuto lavarmi [f].
2   Sandra e Roberto hanno voluto sposarsi.
3   Abbiamo dovuto scusarci [m].
4   Luigi ha dovuto alzarsi alle sei.
5   Gianni non ha voluto mettersi il berretto.
6   Hai potuto curarti [m]?
7   Avete potuto riposarvi [m]?
8   Ho dovuto fermarmi [f].
9   Perché hai voluto tingerti i capelli [m]?
10   Non abbiamo potuto spiegarci [m].

Exercise 5

Translate into Italian, using reflexive/reciprocal pronouns.

1   Are you [pl.] enjoying yourselves?
2   Have you [f] washed your hands?
3   How are you feeling, Madam?
4   You [pl.] are wrong.
5   Where did you [fp] meet?
6   Why don't you [sing.] sit down?
7   Paolo always talks about himself.
8   Franca washed her hair.
9   Carlo apologised.
10   I [f] got dressed.

UNIT TWENTY-ONE
The imperative

1 The imperative is used, in Italian as in English, to express orders, commands or strong requests:

Guarda!	Look!
Entrate!	Come in!
Chiedi a tuo padre.	Ask your father.
Venga domani, Signora!	Come tomorrow, Madam!
Andiamo!	Let's go!
Dammi il libro.	Give me the book.

As well as orders and requests, the imperative can also be used to express wishes, invitations, encouragement and advice:

Passa delle buone vacanze.	Have a good holiday.
Ti ascolto: dimmi tutto.	I'm listening to you: tell me everything.
Non ti preoccupare.	Don't worry.
Hai l'aria stanca: vai a letto!	You look tired: go to bed!

Forms of the imperative

2 Regular verbs in **-are**, **-ere** and **-ire** are conjugated as follows:

	Parlare	*To speak*
(tu)	**parla**	speak
(Lei)	**parli**	speak
(noi)	**parliamo**	let us speak
(voi)	**parlate**	speak
(Loro)	**parlino**	speak

	Prendere	*To take/get*
(tu)	prend*i*	take/get
(Lei)	prend*a*	take/get
(noi)	prend*iamo*	let us take/get
(voi)	prend*ete*	take/get
(Loro)	prend*ano*	take/get

	Partire	*To leave*
(tu)	part*i*	leave
(Lei)	part*a*	leave
(noi)	part*iamo*	let us leave
(voi)	part*ite*	leave
(Loro)	part*ano*	leave

Some verbs ending in **-ire** add **-isc-**, as in the present indicative (see Unit 5):

	Finire	*To finish*
(tu)	fin*isci*	finish
(Lei)	fin*isca*	finish
(noi)	fin*iamo*	let us finish
(voi)	fin*ite*	finish
(Loro)	fin*iscano*	finish

In the first person plural, the meaning is more that of a suggestion than an order, made to a group of which we are part (cf. the English '*Let's* have a coffee'). The third person singular and plural are only used for the polite form.

Parlate con i vostri insegnanti.	Speak to your teachers.
Prendi un analgesico.	Take a painkiller.
Partiamo subito.	Let's leave immediately.
Finisci il compito!	Finish your homework!
Prenda la prima (strada) a destra.	Take the first (street) on the right.

3 Verbs ending in **-care** and **-gare** keep the hard sound of **c** and **g** by adding **h** before the endings of the third person singular (**Lei**) and the first and third persons plural (**noi** and **Loro**):

Cercare	*Pagare*
cerca	paga
cer*chi*	pa*ghi*
cer*chiamo*	pa*ghiamo*
cercate	pagate
cer*chino*	pa*ghino*

Cerchiamo **casa in questa zona!**	Let's look for a flat in this area!
Paghi **il conto, per favore, Signora.**	Pay the bill, please(, Madam).

4 Verbs ending in **-iare** have only one **-i** in the second person singular and the first and third persons plural:

Cominciare	*Mangiare*
comincia	mangia
cominci	mangi
cominciamo	mangiamo
cominciate	mangiate
comincino	mangino

Cominci a lavorare, Signora!	Start working(, Madam)!
Muoio di fame: mangiamo qualcosa!	I'm starving: let's eat something!

Forms of some irregular verbs

5 **Essere** and **avere** are irregular in the imperative:

Essere	*Avere*
sii	abbi
sia	abbia
siamo	abbiamo
siate	abbiate
siano	abbiano

Siate gentili!	Be kind!
Abbi pazienza!	Be patient! [lit. have patience]
Sia pronta per le 10, Signora.	Be ready by 10(, Madam).

6 There are other verbs with irregular imperatives. Here are some of the most common:

Dare	*Dire*	*Fare*
dai/da'*	di'	fai/fa'*
dia	dica	faccia
diamo	diciamo	facciamo
date	dite	fate
diano	dicano	facciano

Stare	*Andare*	*Venire*
stai/sta'*	vai/va'*	vieni
stia	vada	venga
stiamo	andiamo	veniamo
state	andate	venite
stiano	vadano	vengano

Sapere	*Uscire*	*Bere*
sappi	esci	bevi
sappia	esca	beva
sappiamo	usciamo	beviamo
sappiate	uscite	bevete
sappiano	escano	bevano

* The second person singular of these verbs has two forms: the form with the apostrophe is normally used with unstressed pronouns (see paragraph 10).

State attenti!	Pay attention! [lit. be attentive]
Fai/fa' il compito!	Do your homework!
Vieni subito qui!	Come here at once!
Venga avanti, Signora!	Come forward(, Madam)!
Sappi che io non sono d'accordo.	I want you to know that I don't agree. [lit. know that I don't agree]
Di' la verità.	Tell the truth.

7 All verbs ending in **-urre** have the following pattern:

	Tradurre
-uci	traduci
-uca	traduca
-uciamo	traduciamo
-ucete	traducete
-ucano	traducano

Traduciamo insieme queste frasi.	Let's translate these sentences together.
Traduca, per favore.	Translate, please.

Formal form

8 We have already seen the forms used for the polite form. Care must be taken not to confuse imperative and present polite and familiar forms. Compare:

		Imperative	*Present*
familiar	(tu)	**parla**	**parli**
formal	(Lei)	**parli**	**parla**
familiar	(tu)	**leggi**	**leggi**
formal	(Lei)	**legga**	**legge**
familiar	(tu)	**esci/finisci**	**esci/finisci**
formal	(Lei)	**esca/finisca**	**esce/finisce**

Parla col direttore! [familiar imperative]	Speak to the manager!
Parli col direttore, Signora. [formal imperative]	Speak to the manager(, Madam).
Parli col direttore? [familiar present]	Are you speaking to the manager?
Parla col direttore, Signora? [formal present]	Are you speaking to the manager(, Madam)?

In the plural, as usual, the second person is more commonly used than the third:

Parlate col controllore. **(Parlino col controllore.)**	Speak to the conductor.
Abbiate pazienza, Signori. **(Abbiano pazienza, Signori.)**	Be patient, (ladies and) gentlemen.

Negative form

9 For the second person singular, the negative is formed with the infinitive of the verb preceded by **non**. For the other persons, the usual rule applies and **non** precedes the form of the imperative. As an example, here is the negative conjugation of **parlare**:

(tu)	**non parlare**
(Lei)	**non parli**
(noi)	**non parliamo**
(voi)	**non parlate**
(Loro)	**non parlino**

Non essere scortese!	Don't be rude!
Non dite bugie.	Don't tell lies.
Non avere fretta!	Don't rush!

Position of unstressed pronouns

10 When the imperative is used in an affirmative sentence with an unstressed pronoun (direct object, indirect object, reflexive, **ne**, **ci**), the pronoun is always attached to the verb if it is in a second person form (**tu** or **voi**) or the first person plural form (**noi**):

Quel libro è per te: prendi*lo*.	That book is for you: take it.
Chiediamo*le* aiuto.	Let's ask her for help.
Se hai dei problemi, parla*ne*.	If you are having problems, talk about them.
Alzate*vi*, ragazzi!	Get up, boys!
Telefona*gli* (*or* Telefona *loro* – see Unit 10, paragraph 2).	Phone them.

Note that when an unstressed pronoun is used with the forms **da'**, **fa'**, **di'**, **sta'** and **va'** (see paragraph 6), the first consonant of the pronoun (except **gli**) is doubled:

Se sai la verità, di*lla*!	If you know the truth, tell it!
Da*mmi* la penna!	Give me the pen!
Da*nne* un po' a tuo fratello.	Give some to your brother.
Fa*mmi* un piacere.	Do me a favour.
Va*llo* a comprare!	Go and buy it!
Va*cci* subito.	Go there at once.
Di*lle* la verità.	Tell her the truth.
Di*gli* la verità.	Tell him the truth.

In negative sentences, there is an extra option: the pronoun can be placed before the verb (and after **non**):

Non *lo* prendere! *or* **Non prender*lo*!**	Don't take it!
Non *le* chiediamo aiuto. *or* **Non chiediamo*le* aiuto.**	Let's not ask her for help.
Non *ne* parlare! *or* **Non parlar*ne*!**	Don't talk about it!
Non *vi* alzate! *or* **Non alzate*vi*!**	Don't get up!

11 In the polite form (third person singular and plural, **Lei** and **Loro**), the pronouns are *always* placed before the verb:

Quel libro è per Lei: *lo* prenda.	That book is for you: take it.
***Le* scriva una mail.**	Write her an email.
***Ne* parlino al controllore.**	Speak to the conductor about it.
***Si* alzi, Signora!**	Get up(, Madam)!

Exercise 1

Supply the imperative of the verb in brackets.

Example: (tu pagare) il conto: paga

1 (tu comprare) il pane.
2 (noi uscire) subito.
3 (Lei stare) tranquilla, Signora!
4 (tu mettere) in ordine!
5 (voi essere) gentili.
6 (Lei venire), Professore!
7 (tu dare) una mano a tuo fratello.
8 (tu finire) i compiti.
9 (comprare) questa borsa, Signora!
10 (noi fare) una pausa!
11 (tu avere) fiducia in lei.
12 (Lei parlare) più forte, Signora.
13 (tu andare) fuori!
14 (tu dire) tutto quello che sai.
15 (Lei fare) attenzione, Signora.
16 (voi scrivere) le cartoline!
17 (tu fare) attenzione!
18 (Loro entrare), Signori.
19 (voi aprire) le finestre!
20 (tu rispondere) al telefono.

Exercise 2

Supply the polite form for these sentences.

Example: Paga il conto: paghi

1 Chiudi la porta, per favore.
2 Vai al terzo piano.
3 Sorridi!
4 Di' tutto.
5 Fai presto!
6 Sii paziente!
7 Traduci, per favore.
8 Accendi la luce.
9 Stai fermo!
10 Entra!

Exercise 3

Change the imperatives into the negative.

Examples: Dormi!: Non dormire! Alzati!: Non alzarti! *or* Non ti alzare!

1 Partite subito!
2 Rispondi alla sua domanda.
3 Andate in discoteca.
4 Scenda, Signora.
5 Usciamo!
6 Finisci i biscotti.
7 Ascolta!
8 Prenda quella strada!
9 Telefona a Giuseppe.
10 Di' quello che pensi.
11 Tagliati i capelli.
12 Dalle il libro.
13 Parlagli.
14 Scrivetemi.

15 Dillo!
16 Invitali.
17 Prendilo.

18 Mettiti il berretto.
19 Portatele dei fiori.
20 Fallo!

Exercise 4

Change the imperatives into the affirmative.

Examples: Non parlate!: Parlate! Non mi guardare: Guardami!

1   Non andare in piscina.
2   Non prendete l'autobus.
3   Non invitare Giacomo.
4   Non guardiamo quel film.
5   Non cominciare.
6   Non faccia la spesa al mercato.
7   Non mettano l'auto in garage.
8   Non fare così.
9   Non andare al parco.
10 Non stare sul balcone.

11 Non mandarmi una cartolina.
12 Non fatelo.
13 Non darmi i tuoi libri.
14 Non mi rispondere.
15 Non ci andare.
16 Non lo mangiate.
17 Non lo leggete!
18 Non ci aspetti, Professore.
19 Non dirgli il tuo nome.
20 Non darle il tuo indirizzo.

Exercise 5

Change the verb into the imperative, and replace the words in italics with the appropriate pronoun.

Example: Devi dire *la verità*: Dilla.

1   Dovete parlare *a Laura*.
2   Devi prendere *i libri*.
3   Signora, deve firmare *il foglio*.
4   Dovete parlare *del problema*.
5   Dobbiamo andare *al supermercato*.
6   Devi fare *gli esercizi*.
7   Dovete restare *a scuola*.
8   Dobbiamo chiedere *il permesso*.
9   Devi correggere *gli sbagli*.
10 Dovete prendere *il treno*.

11 Signori, devono aspettare *il tram*.
12 Devi mandare *gli auguri*.
13 Dovete comprare *la frutta*.
14 Signor Rossi, deve portare *una foto*.
15 Dovete aiutare *i vostri amici*.
16 Devi rendere *il libro*.
17 Dobbiamo chiedere *a Lina*.
18 Devi telefonare *ai nonni*.
19 Devi bere *del caffè*.
20 Dovete studiare *filosofia*.

UNIT TWENTY-TWO
The pronoun **si**

The pronoun **si** is used as an impersonal subject, either in sentences without a specified subject, or in sentences with a passive meaning. In both, it is always put before the verb.

Si in sentences where the subject is not specified

1 **Si** is used as an impersonal subject in sentences where the subject is not specified. It corresponds to the English 'one' or 'you' (as in 'One never knows/You never know what's just round the corner'), or 'they', meaning a number of unspecified people (as in 'They eat kangaroo in Australia'). When **si** is used in this way, the verb is always in the third person singular:

Si esce **da questa porta.**	You go out by this door.
'Sono stato al mare.' 'Si vede: sei abbronzato!'	'I've been at the seaside.' 'It shows [lit. one sees]: you've got a tan!'
Si paga **alla cassa.**	You pay/One pays at the till.
C'è stato un incidente e non *si passa.*	There's been an accident and you can't get through.
All'ostello della gioventù *si spende* **meno.**	You spend less in a youth hostel.
Per andare al museo si *passa* **da piazza Garibaldi.**	To get to the museum you go through piazza Garibaldi.

As the examples suggest, **si** is often used for rules or general advice.

2 With verbs like **essere**, **diventare**, **sembrare**, etc., followed by a noun or an adjective, **si** requires the noun to be plural (even though the verb is always singular), and the adjective to be masculine plural:

Quando *si è* **studenti** *si è* **poveri.**	When one is a student, one is poor.
Se si mangia troppo *si diventa* **grassi.**	If you eat too much you get fat.
Quando *si è* **malati si rimane a casa.**	When you are ill you stay at home.
Quando *si è* **giovani si è ottimisti.**	When one is young one is an optimist.
Se si veste in nero *si sembra* **magri.**	If you dress in black you look slim.

Si in sentences with a passive meaning

3 **Si** is also used as an impersonal subject in sentences which have a passive meaning, like this one: 'In Nuova Zelanda si parla inglese.' The corresponding sentence in English would have either a passive verb ('English is spoken in New Zealand') or an impersonal one ('One speaks/They speak English in New Zealand').

In this type of sentence, the verb can be in either the third person singular or the third person plural. The singular is used if the noun that accompanies the verb is singular:

Il biglietto [sing.] **si** *prende* **all'ingresso.**	The ticket is obtained/You get your ticket at the door.
Il sale [sing.] **si** *compra* **in tabaccheria.**	Salt is bought/You buy salt at the tobacconist's.
Al mercato si *vende la frutta* [sing.] **migliore.**	The best fruit is sold at the market.
Si *deve* **lavare** *l'insalata* [sing.] **prima di mangiarla.**	Lettuce should be washed before you eat it/You should wash lettuce before eating it.
In biblioteca si *può* **leggere** *il giornale* [sing.].	In the library you can read the paper/ The paper can be read in the library.

The plural is used when the noun that accompanies the verb is plural:

Anche *le cartoline* [pl.] **si** *comprano* **in tabaccheria.**	Postcards are also bought/You also buy postcards at the tobacconist's.
I lamponi [pl.] **si** *mangiano* **in estate.**	Raspberries are eaten in summer.
In vacanza si *fanno* **molte** *fotografie* [pl.].	A lot of pictures are taken on holiday/ On holiday you take a lot of pictures.
Si *devono* **comprare** *i biglietti* [pl.] **in anticipo.**	Tickets should be purchased in advance.
In quel Cine Club si *possono* **vedere** *molti film* [pl.].	A lot of films can be seen/You can see a lot of films at that cine club.

Negative form

4 The negative is formed by putting **non** before the pronoun:

Non si fuma in aereo.	There's no smoking [lit. one does not smoke] in planes.
Non si devono aprire le finestre.	The windows mustn't be opened/One mustn't open the windows.

Si used with the auxiliary *essere*

5 When **si** occurs with a verb in the present perfect (or any compound tense), the auxiliary is **essere**; the past participle must therefore agree with the subject of the passive verb:

Su questo argomento si *sono* scritt*i* molti libri.	Many books have been written on this subject.
In Piemonte si *è* sempre prodott*o* del buon vino.	In Piedmont good wine has always been produced/they have always produced good wine.
In questa scuola si *sono* sempre cominciat*e* le lezioni alle 8.	In this school lessons have always (been) started at eight o'clock.
Quando si *è* finit*a* l'università si cerca lavoro.	When university has been finished/ When you have finished university, you look for a job.

The same applies when **si** is not used in a passive function, but purely as an impersonal subject ('one', 'you', 'they', etc.):

Quando non si è riusciti a risolvere un problema, non si è soddisfatti.	When one hasn't managed to solve a problem, one is dissatisfied.
Dopo che si è stati malati, si è sempre deboli.	You're always weak when you've been ill.

Si used with reflexive verbs

6 When **si** is used with a reflexive verb, the reflexive or reciprocal pronoun is **ci**, not **si**; the resulting form is thus **ci si**:

A volte in vacanza ci si annoia.	Sometimes you get bored on holiday.
Se in vacanza *ci si* è annoiati, si è contenti di tornare a scuola.	If you've been bored in the holidays, you're glad to go back to school.

Quando *ci si* alza presto la giornata   When you get up early, the day seems
   sembra troppo lunga!   too long!

Exercise 1

Complete the sentences with the correct form of the verb.

> Examples: Dal balcone si (vedere) le montagne: vedono; A Natale si
> (mangiare) il panettone: mangia

1 Si (fare) attenzione quando si (attraversare) la strada.
2 In Svizzera si (parlare) tre lingue.
3 Di domenica non si (lavorare).
4 Negli uffici pubblici non si (fumare).
5 Si (dovere) aiutare gli anziani.
6 In quella discoteca non si (entrare) con le scarpe da ginnastica.
7 Certi segreti non si (potere) mantenere.
8 Per entrare nel centro della città si (pagare) un pedaggio.
9 In quel bosco si (trovare) molti funghi.
10 Al mercato si (comprare) la verdura più fresca.

Exercise 2

Rewrite the sentences with the correct form of the verbs and the adjectives or
nouns in brackets.

> Examples: Quando si (essere malato), si (andare) a letto: Quando si è
> malati, si va a letto; Quando si (essere studente), si (dovere)
> studiare: Quando si è studenti, si deve studiare.

1 Quando si (avere) freddo, (lavorare) male.
2 Quando si (avere) la febbre, si (restare) a casa.
3 Quando si (cominciare) a studiare una lingua, si (fare) degli sbagli.
4 Quando si (guidare) non si (usare) il cellulare.
5 Quando si (avere) fame si (mangiare).
6 Quando si (essere stanco) si (fare) molti sbagli.
7 Quando si (essere avvocato) si (conoscere) la legge.
8 Quando non si (avere) soldi, non si (fare) spese inutili.
9 Quando si (avere) tanti amici si (essere fortunato).
10 Quando si (mangiare) troppi dolci, si (ingrassare).

Exercise 3

Change the sentences into impersonal form by using the pronoun **si**.

Examples: Non devi mangiare con le mani: Non si mangia con le mani;
Non devi raccogliere i fiori: Non si raccolgono i fiori.

1   Non devi mettere i piedi sulla scrivania.
2   La mattina devi fare colazione.
3   Dopo pranzo devi lavare i piatti.
4   Non devi parlare con gli sconosciuti.
5   Non devi andare in bicicletta sul marciapiedi.
6   Non devi mangiare durante le lezioni.
7   Non devi guardarti tanto allo specchio.
8   In biblioteca devi parlare a bassa voce.
9   Non devi guardare la televisione tutto il giorno.
10   Il giorno prima degli esami devi studiare.

Exercise 4

Change the sentences into impersonal form by using the pronoun **si**. Pay attention to the use of the past tense.

Example: Quando/Dopo che hai parcheggiato l'auto in salita, devi
mettere il freno a mano: Quando/Dopo che si è parcheggiata
l'auto in salita, si deve mettere il freno a mano.

1   Dopo che hai fatto il bagno in mare, fai la doccia.
2   Dopo che hai superato un esame, sei contento.
3   Dopo che hai finito di lavorare, vai a casa.
4   Dopo che sei salito sull'aereo, non puoi usare il cellulare.
5   Quando sei cresciuto in campagna, conosci i nomi di tante piante.

UNIT TWENTY-THREE
The present conditional

Use of the present conditional

1 The present conditional expresses an action which depends on a condition, as in this English example: 'If I *could*, I *would go* at once.' In this example, the condition is expressed with 'if' (i.e. 'on condition that'). The present conditional is often used even when the condition is not actually mentioned, as in: 'I'm sure she *would love* a night out.' Basically, the use of the Italian present conditional is similar to the English:

Vorrei **ballare tutta la sera.**	I would like to dance all night.
Mi *daresti* **un passaggio?**	Would you give me a lift?
Fareste **meglio restare a casa.**	You'd do better to stay at home.

The present conditional in Italian can express wishes or intentions, opinions or advice, requests in polite form, doubts and conjectures:

Prenderei un caffè.	I'd like a coffee.
Potreste andare a piedi.	You could go on foot.
Mi daresti una mano?	Would/could you give me a hand?
Sapresti fare questo lavoro?	Would you know how to do that job?
Questa potrebbe essere la soluzione.	This could be the solution.

The forms of the present conditional

2 The present conditional is formed in the same way as the future, but with different endings:

	-*are*	-*ere*	-*ire*
(io)	-erei	-erei	-irei
(tu)	-eresti	-eresti	-iresti
(lui/lei)	-erebbe	-erebbe	-irebbe
(noi)	-eremmo*	-eremmo*	-iremmo*
(voi)	-ereste	-ereste	-ireste
(loro)	-erebbero	-erebbero	-irebbero

* Be sure not to confuse the spelling of these endings (all with **-emmo**) with the corresponding ones of the future (all with **-emo**).

Regular verbs ending in **-are** are conjugated as follows:

Parlare	*To speak*
parlerei	I would speak
parleresti	you would speak
parlerebbe	he/she/it would speak
parleremmo	we would speak
parlereste	you would speak
parlerebbero	they would speak

Regular verbs ending in **-ere** are conjugated as follows:

Prendere	*To take/get*
prenderei	I would take
prenderesti	you would take
prenderebbe	he/she/it would take
prenderemmo	we would take
prendereste	you would take
prenderebbero	they would take

Regular verbs ending in **-ire** are conjugated as follows:

Finire	*To finish*
finirei	I would finish
finiresti	you would finish
finirebbe	he/she/it would finish
finiremmo	we would finish
finireste	you would finish
finirebbero	they would finish

Con Marco *parleresti* **italiano.**	With Marco you would speak Italian.
Scriverei **una cartolina alla zia.**	I would write a postcard to my aunt.
Finiremmo **questo lavoro prima di partire.**	We'd finish this job before leaving.

3 Verbs ending in **-care** and **-gare** add **h** before the endings of the present conditional in order to keep the hard sound of **c** and **g**:

Cercare	*Pagare*
cer*ch*erei	pa*gh*erei
cer*ch*eresti	pa*gh*eresti
cer*ch*erebbe	pa*gh*erebbe
cer*ch*eremmo	pa*gh*eremmo
cer*ch*ereste	pa*gh*ereste
cer*ch*erebbero	pa*gh*erebbero

Al suo posto, *cercherei* **un altro lavoro.**	If I were him [lit. in his place], I'd look for another job.
La Signora *pagherebbe* **il conto.**	The lady would pay the bill.

4 Verbs ending in **-ciare** and **-giare** drop **-i** in the present conditional:

Cominciare	*Mangiare*
comin*c*erei	man*g*erei
comin*c*eresti	man*g*eresti
comin*c*erebbe	man*g*erebbe
comin*c*eremmo	man*g*eremmo
comin*c*ereste	man*g*ereste
comin*c*erebbero	man*g*erebbero

Senza di lui, non *cominceremmo* **la riunione.**	We wouldn't start the meeting without him.
Mangeresti **la carne di canguro?!**	Would you eat kangaroo meat?!

Present conditional of some irregular verbs

Irregular verbs are grouped in the same way as for the future tense:

5 **Essere** and **avere** are irregular:

Essere	*Avere*
sarei	**avrei**
saresti	**avresti**
sarebbe	**avrebbe**
saremmo	**avremmo**
sareste	**avreste**
sarebbero	**avrebbero**

Sarei **contenta di rivedere Carlo.**	I would be happy to see Carlo again.
Avresti **un minuto per me?**	Could you spare me a minute? [lit. would you have a minute for me?]

6 **Dare**, **fare** and **stare** follow the same pattern as **essere**:

darei	farei	starei
daresti	faresti	staresti
darebbe	farebbe	starebbe
daremmo	faremmo	staremmo
dareste	fareste	stareste
darebbero	farebbero	starebbero

Darei una festa.	I would give a party.
Mi faresti un favore?	Would you do me a favour?
Al posto tuo starei tranquillo.	I wouldn't worry if I were you. [lit. in your place I'd be calm]

7 **Andare**, **cadere**, **dovere**, **potere**, **sapere**, **vedere** and **vivere** follow the same pattern as **avere**:

andrei	cadrei	dovrei	potrei
andresti	cadresti	dovresti	potresti
andrebbe	cadrebbe	dovrebbe	potrebbe
andremmo	cadremmo	dovremmo	potremmo
andreste	cadreste	dovreste	potreste
andrebbero	cadrebbero	dovrebbero	potrebbero

saprei	vedrei	vivrei
sapresti	vedresti	vivresti
saprebbe	vedrebbe	vivrebbe
sapremmo	vedremmo	vivremmo
sapreste	vedreste	vivreste
saprebbero	vedrebbero	vivrebbero

Quando andreste in vacanza?	When would you go on holiday?
Domenica dovrei lavorare.	On Sunday I ought to work.
Potresti aiutarmi!!	You could help me!! [i.e. why aren't you helping me?]

8 A third group of irregular verbs, comprising **bere**, **rimanere**, **venire**, **volere** and **tenere**, have the following pattern:

-rrei	berrei	rimarrei	verrei	vorrei	terrei
-rresti	berresti	rimarresti	verresti	vorresti	terresti
-rrebbe	berrebbe	rimarrebbe	verrebbe	vorrebbe	terrebbe
-rremmo	berremmo	rimarremmo	verremmo	vorremmo	terremmo
-rreste	berreste	rimarreste	verreste	vorreste	terreste
-rrebbero	berrebbero	rimarrebbero	verrebbero	vorrebbero	terrebbero

Rimarrei ancora un po' con voi, ma devo prendere il treno.	I would stay with you a bit longer, but I've got to get the train.
Verresti al cinema con me?	Would you come to the cinema with me?
Vorrei un caffè.*	I'd like a coffee.
Vorrei anche un chilo di mele.*	I'd like a kilo of apples as well.

* The present conditional of **volere** is often used to expresses wishes and requests in a polite form, corresponding to the English 'would like'.

9 All verbs ending in **-urre** have the following pattern:

-urrei	**tradurrei**
-urresti	**tradurresti**
-urrebbe	**tradurrebbe**
-urremmo	**tradurremmo**
-urreste	**tradurreste**
-urrebbero	**tradurrebbero**

L'interprete tradurrebbe tutto per te.	The interpreter would translate everything for you.

Negative form

10 The negative is formed by putting **non** before the verb:

Non capiresti nulla.	You wouldn't understand a thing.
Non vorremmo partire.	We wouldn't want to leave.
Non tradurrei così.	I wouldn't translate (it) like that.

Exercise 1

Supply the present conditional of the verb in brackets.

Example: Stasera non (io uscire): uscirei

1 (tu leggere) quel libro di nuovo?!
2 (io potere) aiutarvi.
3 (voi avere) voglia di uscire?
4 Mi (tu svegliare)?
5 (loro volere) venire a cena.
6 (tu pagare) anche per me?
7 Non (io fare) quel lavoro.
8 (noi dovere) studiare.
9 (tu sapere) guidare un trattore?
10 Claudia (rimanere) a casa.
11 Al posto tuo non (io aprire) la porta.

12 (tu dovere) telefonare a Pia.
13 A Liz (piacere) vivere in Italia.
14 Mi (potere) aspettare, Signora?
15 Mauro (essere) la persona giusta.
16 Mi (voi dare) un passaggio?
17 (io bere) volentieri qualcosa.
18 Non (loro abitare) mai in una casa come questa.
19 Chi (tradurre) dall'arabo?
20 (tu accompagnare) Silvia alla stazione?

Exercise 2

Rewrite the sentences, changing the italicised verbs into the present conditional.

   Example: *Veniamo* volentieri: Verremmo volentieri.

1 *Voglio* due panini.
2 *Dovete* studiare di più.
3 Lucia *va* in vacanza.
4 *Fate* una pausa?
5 *Possiamo* parlarti?
6 Maurizio *cambia* lavoro.
7 Mi *dai* un consiglio?
8 Vi *piace* andare a Venezia?
9 I nostri amici *devono* arrivare oggi.
10 Non *esce* mai senza permesso.

Exercise 3

Translate into Italian, using the present conditional:

1 Paola could help me.
2 We would gladly come.
3 I wouldn't go to the library in the evenings.
4 When would you start, Signora Vialli?
5 Pietro would like to invite you [sing.] to the party.
6 We'd be happy to see you [pl.].
7 They would keep the dog in the garden.
8 I would have to leave early.
9 I'd like another biscuit.
10 Would you know the result, Mr Spadavecchia?

KEY TO EXERCISES

UNIT 1

Exercise 1

1 m   2 f   3 m   4 f   5 f   6 m   7 m   8 m   9 m   10 m/f   11 m   12 f
13 m/f   14 m   15 f   16 f   17 m/f   18 m   19 m   20 f

Exercise 2

1 ragazzi   2 marche   3 chiavi   4 abitanti   5 zii   6 fiumi   7 stazioni
8 ragazze   9 energie   10 pomeriggi   11 banche   12 pianisti   13 clienti
14 indirizzi   15 occhi   16 ristoranti   17 televisioni   18 calendari
19 francesi   20 laghi

Exercise 3

1 nome   2 via   3 figlio   4 mano   5 opinione   6 cliente   7 occhio   8 persona   9 marca   10 problema   11 ciliegia   12 caffè   13 medico
14 attivista   15 ginocchio   16 bugia   17 tedesco   18 test   19 uomo
20 amica

UNIT 2

Exercise 1

1 la   2 la   3 il   4 la   5 l' *or* le   6 il   7 i   8 l'   9 lo   10 gli   11 le
12 lo *or* gli   13 l'   14 la   15 la *or* le   16 gli   17 le   18 le   19 la *or* le
20 l'

Exercise 2

1 una   2 una   3 un   4 uno   5 una   6 un   7 un'   8 una   9 un   10 uno

11 un'   12 uno   13 una   14 un'   15 uno   16 un   17 uno   18 un
19 uno   20 un'

Exercise 3

1 lo   2 una   3 le   4 un'   5 la   6 il   7 un'   8 l', un   9 il   10 lo

UNIT 3

Exercise 1

1 interessante   2 bianca   3 bianchi   4 rosse   5 egoisti   6 bell'
7 razzista   8 comiche   9 simpatiche   10 lunghi   11 quel, simpatico
12 questi, facili   13 quei, begli   14 queste, belle   15 quegli, morti
16 questi, inglesi   17 quelle, spagnole   18 quel, bell'   19 quelle, fresche
20 quei, greci

Exercise 2

1 grande   2 rosa   3 francesi   4 grave   5 pacifisti   6 tedesche   7 pigro
8 lunghi   9 belghe   10 belga   11 sporche   12 energico   13 resistenti
14 blu   15 scozzesi   16 veloci   17 simpatiche   18 italiani   19 ottimisti
20 soddisfatti

Exercise 3

1 i loro   2 i suoi   3 la mia   4 le tue   5 la vostra   6 il nostro   7 i miei   8 la
loro   9 tua   10 la Sua

Exercise 4

1 il suo   2 la nostra   3 i tuoi   4 il mio   5 i suoi   6 le tue *or* le Sue   7 la
loro   8 i vostri *or* i Loro   9 le sue   10 i nostri

Exercise 5

1 questi, i nostri, tedeschi   2 i Suoi, ottimisti   3 queste, le vostre   4 i miei, i
Suoi   5 questi, i miei, quelli, i tuoi   6 il nostro, entusiasta, il vostro
7 quelle, le mie, queste, le tue   8 quegli, divertenti, questo, difficile 9 i miei,
pesanti, i vostri, leggeri   10 quell', minerale, gassata, questa, liscia

UNIT 4

Exercise 1

1 siamo   2 sei   3 sono   4 sono   5 siete   6 è   7 è   8 sono   9 siete
10 siamo   11 sono   12 siete   13 è   14 sono   15 sei   16 è   17 è
18 sono   19 siete   20 è

Exercise 2

1 abbiamo   2 ha   3 ho   4 hanno   5 avete   6 ha   7 ha   8 hai
9 abbiamo   10 hai   11 avete   12 ha   13 abbiamo   14 hanno   15 hai
16 ha   17 hanno   18 hai   19 ho   20 ha

Exercise 3

1 Non ho ragione; Ho ragione?   2 Il professore non ha caldo; Il professore
ha caldo?   3 La Signorina Berti non ha sete; La Signorina Berti ha sete?
4 Lei non ha sonno; Lei ha sonno?   5 Non avete paura; Avete paura?
6 Non hanno freddo; Hanno freddo?   7 Carla e Andrea non hanno fame;
Carla e Andrea hanno fame?

Exercise 4

1 Sono stanco; Non sono stanco.   2 Sei pigra; Non sei pigra.   3 Il dottore è
giovane; Il dottore non è giovane.   4 La professoressa è simpatica; La professoressa non è simpatica.   5 Lei è alto; Lei non è alto.   6 Siamo magre; Non
siamo magre.   7 Siete intelligenti; Non siete intelligenti.   8 Le tue amiche
sono contente; Le tue amiche non sono contente.

Exercise 5

1 Nell'ufficio c'è una sedia.   2 Nell'ufficio ci sono due poltrone.   3 Nell'ufficio ci sono tre computer.   4 Nell'ufficio c'è una stampante.   5 Nell'ufficio
c'è un telefono.   6 Nell'ufficio c'è la fotocopiatrice.   7 Nell'ufficio ci sono
due radiatori.   8 Nell'ufficio c'è una porta.   9 Nell'ufficio ci sono tre
finestre.

Exercise 6

1 In questo paese c'è un museo, ci sono tre musei, non ci sono musei.   2 In
questo paese c'è una discoteca, ci sono due discoteche, non ci sono discoteche.   3 In questo paese c'è una panetteria, ci sono quattro panetterie, non
ci sono panetterie.   4 In questo paese c'è un cinema, ci sono due cinema,
non ci sono cinema.   5 In questo paese c'è una biblioteca, ci sono due

biblioteche, non ci sono biblioteche.   6 In questo paese c'è una scuola, ci sono due scuole, non ci sono scuole.   7 In questo paese c'è un ufficio postale, ci sono due uffici postali, non ci sono uffici postali.   8 In questo paese c'è una libreria, ci sono quattro librerie, non ci sono librerie.   9 In questo paese c'è un giardino pubblico, ci sono tre giardini pubblici, non ci sono giardini pubblici.   10 In questo paese c'è un ristorante, ci sono sei ristoranti, non ci sono ristoranti.

UNIT 5

Exercise 1

1 arriva   2 vive   3 mangiamo   4 cerchi   5 prendete   6 parte   7 leggiamo   8 pulisci   9 conosco   10 finiscono   11 guidiamo   12 giochiamo   13 tornate   14 capisci   15 spendono   16 abita   17 pagate   18 viaggi   19 ricevi   20 lasciano

Exercise 2

1 vanno   2 produce   3 diamo   4 vai   5 fate   6 riusciamo   7 venite   8 posso   9 vogliono   10 dici   11 potete   12 voglio   13 stai   14 sanno   15 fanno   16 devono   17 traduciamo   18 deve   19 sapete   20 vengono

Exercise 3

1 Dovete parlare con Marcello.   2 Partiamo stasera.   3 Prendiamo il prossimo autobus.   4 (Lei) può andare al cinema, Signor Buchan.   5 Sappiamo usare quei cellulari.   6 Preferisce sempre leggere il giornale.   7 Il bambino dorme.   8 Vengo a Torino quest'estate.   9 Escono spesso la sera.   10 I ragazzi giocano a pallone domani.

Exercise 4

1 Esci stasera, mamma?   2 Cosa facciamo domani?   3 Puoi aprire quella porta?   4 Vuoi un caffè?   5 Sai suonare il piano, Francesco?   6 Cosa cerchi?   7 (Lei) beve caffè o acqua minerale, Signora?   8 Tu e Jim conoscete i miei genitori?   9 Stai bene oggi?   10 Cosa costruiscono?

Exercise 5

1 (Lei) non parla inglese, Signora Vialli?   2 I miei amici tedeschi non sanno cantare in italiano.   3 Non guadagno molto.   4 Non dà una festa per il suo compleanno?   5 Non lavori con Giulia?   6 Non vedono il Signor Moro da tre anni.   7 Perché non vai mai a Firenze, Claudio?   8 Non riesco a chiudere

questa finestra.   9 Perché non bevete caffè stamattina?   10 Non venite domani?

UNIT 6

Exercise 1

1 dolcemente   2 tranquillamente   3 semplicemente   4 allegramente
5 maggiormente   6 irregolarmente   7 probabilmente   8 chiaramente
9 facilmente   10 velocemente   11 lentamente   12 utilmente
13 attentamente   14 rapidamente   15 leggermente

Exercise 2

1 molti   2 molto   3 pochi   4 troppo   5 troppi   6 tanta   7 troppo
8 molto   9 poco   10 molte   11 poco   12 molto   13 molto   14 pochi
15 molto   16 poca   17 molta   18 molto   19 troppe   20 poche

Exercise 3

1 con prudenza   2 con pazienza   3 in modo nervoso   4 a poco a poco
5 senza esitazione   6 di solito   7 in tempo   8 con coraggio   9 di sicuro
10 in maniera brusca

Exercise 4

1 A volte mangio in mensa.   2 La piscina è abbastanza grande.   3 Usciamo spesso con i nostri amici.   4 Hai abbastanza soldi?   5 Devi parlare lentamente *or* piano.   6 Marina non mangia mai (il) formaggio.   7 Francesca arriva sempre tardi *or* in ritardo.   8 Aspetto da quasi quaranta minuti! 9 Carla e Andrea sono fuori.   10 I tuoi genitori stanno bene?

UNIT 7

Exercise 1

1 Anna la guarda.   2 Li invitiamo.   3 Le scrivete?   4 Lo leggono.   5 La suono.   6 La preparo.   7 Lo chiamo.   8 Li faccio.   9 Le invito.   10 Le chiudete.   11 Lorenzo li corregge.   12 Lo prendono.   13 Li porto.   14 Li cerco.   15 Pia la beve.   16 Paola lo finisce.   17 Li accompagno.   18 Le vedi oggi?   19 La ascolto.   20 Luca li lava.

Exercise 2

1 Non le voglio.   2 Non li compriamo.   3 Non ci chiamano.   4 Silvia non li invita?   5 I Signori Bianchi non lo prendono.   6 Non mi invitate?   7 Non vi aspetto.   8 Non la vedo domani.   9 Non ti accompagno alla stazione. 10 Non lo guardiamo.

Exercise 3

1 Vogliamo vederlo.   2 Non posso aiutarti.   3 Puoi accompagnarmi? 4 Vuoi sentirla?   5 Devono chiamarci.   6 Voglio invitarvi.   7 Vuole conoscerle.   8 Non potete farli.   9 Devi ascoltarmi.   10 Non posso aiutarLa, Signora.

Exercise 4

1 lo   2 le   3 li   4 li   5 la   6 mi   7 li   8 La   9 li   10 le   11 la   12 li 13 la   14 vi   15 lo   16 la   17 la   18 li   19 le   20 lo

Exercise 5

1 Vi invitiamo alla festa.   2 Ho molti amici e li vedo spesso.   3 Signora Fusi, La posso chiamare *or* posso chiamarLa domani?   4 Ci aiuti la settimana prossima?   5 Ti devo vedere *or* Devo vederti.   6 Olga e Anna partono domani e le voglio accompagnare/portare *or* voglio accompagnarle/portarle alla stazione.   7 Non vi posso aiutare *or* non posso aiutarvi.   8 'Porti la chitarra?' 'No, non ce l'ho.'   9 Tullio compra queste riviste e le legge.   10 Mi puoi portare/accompagnare *or* puoi portarmi/accompagnarmi a scuola domani?

UNIT 8

Exercise 1

1 della mamma   2 dello zio   3 degli amici   4 del parco   5 dell'auto   6 dei paesi   7 delle stanze   8 al mare   9 allo stadio   10 alla stazione   11 ai ragazzi   12 agli uomini   13 alle donne   14 all'ospedale   15 dalla zia 16 dallo studente   17 dal dentista   18 dall'aeroporto   19 dagli uffici 20 dalle colleghe   21 dai ministri   22 nell'albergo   23 nello stipendio 24 nella casa   25 negli anni   26 nei cassetti   27 nelle camere   28 nel frigo   29 sul tavolo   30 sulla sedia   31 sullo scaffale   32 sulle spalle 33 sui libri   34 sugli alberi   35 sull'idea

Exercise 2

1 a   2 in   3 al   4 fra *or* tra   5 da   6 alla   7 con   8 dal   9 del   10 ai
11 a, in   12 al, con   13 nel   14 alle   15 da   16 alle   17 per   18 con
19 del   20 a

Exercise 3

1 a   2 in   3 a, in   4 a   5 di   6 al   7 a   8 a   9 da, a   10 da   11 a
12 in   13 in   14 alla   15 a *or* per   16 al   17 della   18 in   19 nella   20 di

Exercise 4

1 Finisco di lavorare alle 6.   2 Antonio parte per Genova.   3 Gemma è nata
nel 2001.   4 Fabia non esce mai di sera.   5 I Signori Bancroft abitano in
campagna, in una vecchia villa.   6 La biblioteca è dietro la palestra.   7 Non
puoi uscire senza di me!   8 Abitate lontano dalla scuola?   9 La zia di Isabella vive a Greve, in Toscana.   10 Ha una gonna di pelle.   11 Angus è di
Edimburgo, in Scozia.   12 Deve girare a destra dopo la chiesa(, Signora).
13 Stasera mangiamo in pizzeria.   14 Questi fiori sono per tua madre.   15 A
or per Natale andiamo a sciare in montagna.   16 Abito vicino alla pri-
gione.   17 Margaret vive a Torino da cinque anni.   18 Il treno per Aosta
parte dal binario 7.   19 Regaliamo *or* diamo a Luisa un CD di musica
russa.   20 Compro sempre il pane da Belli.

UNIT 9

Exercise 1

1 chi   2 chi   3 chi   4 che *or* cosa *or* che cosa   5 che *or* cosa *or* che cosa
6 chi   7 chi   8 che *or* cosa *or* che cosa   9 chi   10 che *or* cosa *or* che cosa
11 chi   12 che *or* cosa *or* che cosa   13 chi   14 chi   15 che *or* cosa *or* che
cosa   16 chi   17 che *or* cosa *or* che cosa   18 chi   19 che *or* cosa *or* che
cosa   20 chi

Exercise 2

1 dove   2 quando   3 perché   4 come   5 quando   6 che   7 che *or* quale
8 dov'   9 perché   10 qual   11 che *or* quale   12 che *or* quale   13 come
14 dove   15 perché   16 dov'   17 quando   18 qual   19 perché   20 che *or*
quali

Exercise 3

1 quante   2 quanto   3 quanti   4 quanti   5 quante   6 quanta   7 quanto
8 quante   9 quanti   10 quanto   11 quanta   12 quanto   13 quanti
14 quanto   15 quanto   16 quante   17 quanto   18 quante   19 quanti
20 quanto

Exercise 4

1 Quanti panini volete?   2 Dove andate a pranzo?   3 Chi sono quelle persone?   4 Che/Cosa/Che cosa fai domenica?   5 Quando andate in vacanza?
6 Perché Luisa non parte?   7 Qual è la tua bici?   8 Che/Quale film guardi?
9 Chi di loro è italiano/italiana?   10 Quando arriva il treno?

UNIT 10

Exercise 1

1 Le telefoniamo.   2 Gli spedisco *or* spedisco loro le cartoline.   3 Silvia gli racconta una storia.   4 Le regalo un libro.   5 Anna gli scrive *or* scrive loro.
6 Le porto i fiori.   7 Gli scriviamo *or* scriviamo loro.   8 Olga e Silvia le parlano.   9 Gli legge *or* legge loro un libro.   10 Cosa gli regalate?

Exercise 2

1 Non le parlo di lavoro.   2 Non mi telefoni?   3 Non vi regalo dei libri.
4 Non gli offrite qualcosa?   5 Gli amici non le offrono un gelato.   6 Non ci scrivete?   7 Non ti mando una cartolina.   8 Non vi restituisco il libro.
9 Paolo non mi dice la verità.   10 Non gli spedisco il pacco.

Exercise 3

1 Possiamo scriverle?   2 Devo parlarti.   3 Voglio regalargli una chitarra.
4 Puoi telefonarci?   5 Devono offrirvi qualcosa!   6 Potete dirmi tutto.
7 Posso parlarLe, Signora?   8 Non dovete scrivergli.   9 Non posso risponderti.   10 Voglio crederle.

Exercise 4

1 le   2 ti   3 gli   4 gli   5 Le   6 vi   7 ci   8 ti   9 gli   10 Le   11 mi   12 le
13 gli   14 gli   15 vi   16 gli   17 mi   18 le   19 ti   20 gli

Exercise 5

1 Puoi dire a Lucia che le voglio parlare *or* voglio parlarle? 2 Appena arrivo a Roma vi telefono. 3 Devo chiederLe *or* Le devo chiedere un favore, Signora. 4 Gli dai il tuo numero di telefono? 5 Ci dicono *or* raccontano sempre (delle) cose interessanti. 6 Mi mandano sempre una cartolina, quando vanno in Italia. 7 Per il suo compleanno le dò dei fiori. 8 Devo darti *or* ti devo dare i libri di Luca. 9 Se volete vi racconto una storia. 10 Massimo mi scrive ogni settimana *or* tutte le settimane.

UNIT 11

Exercise 1

1 Non le piacciono i carciofi. 2 Non gli piace guidare. 3 Gli piace viaggiare. 4 Gli piace il mare. 5 Gli piace ballare. 6 Non ci piace il pesce. 7 Vi piace nuotare? 8 Le piacciono i film francesi. 9 Non le piace stirare. 10 Gli piace andare in moto.

Exercise 2

1 Non le piace andare in centro il sabato. 2 Non ti piace la musica classica? 3 Non gli piacciono i funghi. 4 Non vi piace guardare la televisione? 5 Non mi piacciono i film di fantascienza. 6 Non gli piace la scuola. 7 Non ci piacciono le canzoni italiane. 8 Non le piacciono gli spaghetti. 9 Non mi piace sciare. 10 Non vi piace la cioccolata al latte?

Exercise 3

1 (Non) mi piace la frutta. 2 (Non) mi piace il calcio. 3 (Non) mi piacciono le fragole. 4 (Non) mi piace giocare a tennis. 5 (Non) mi piace uscire con gli amici. 6 (Non) mi piacciono i gatti. 7 (Non) mi piace la pizza. 8 (Non) mi piacciono i dolci. 9 (Non) mi piace ballare. 10 (Non) mi piacciono le vacanze.

Exercise 4

1 A Luigi (non) piace il caffè senza zucchero. 2 Al professore (non) piacciono le poesie di Leopardi. 3 A mia sorella (non) piace andare al cinema. 4 Ai miei cugini (non) piacciono i film di Fellini. 5 Al primo ministro (non) piace la politica.

Exercise 5

1 basta   2 sembra   3 piacciono   4 manca   5 servono   6 mancano
7 sembra   8 servono   9 pare   10 bastano

Exercise 6

1 Un'ora non mi basta!   2 A Giovanni serve una penna.   3 A Lynne mancano gli *or* i suoi amici italiani.   4 Ti piace la cioccolata *or* il cioccolato?
5 Non le piace andare al cinema.   6 Vi serve un passaggio?   7 Gli servono
una penna e un quaderno.   8 Le sembra noioso lo spettacolo, Signora?
9 Ti serve aiuto? 10 Mi piace leggere.

UNIT 12

Exercise 1

1 restati   2 uscite   3 andata   4 arrivati   5 entrata   6 riuscito   7 arrivato
8 piaciuta   9 costati   10 nata

Exercise 2

1 hai comprato   2 ha regalato   3 siamo andati *or* andate   4 avete trovato
5 hai spento   6 è venuta   7 ha portato   8 avete preso   9 ho visto   10 hai
potuto   11 ho dovuto   12 è uscito, ha perso   13 ha scritto   14 abbiamo
giocato   15 ha cominciato   16 ha voluto *or* è voluto   17 hai messo   18 hai
potuto   19 avete avuto   20 hai letto

Exercise 3

1 abbiamo dovuto   2 avete mangiato   3 sei partito *or* partita   4 ha telefonato   5 ha voluto *or* è voluta   6 hai conosciuto   7 ha dovuto *or* è
dovuta   8 avete accompagnato   9 ha vinto   10 hai finito   11 ho capito
12 hai portato   13 siamo riusciti *or* riuscite   14 avete deciso   15 ha avuto
16 sono venuti   17 avete fatto   18 è partito   19 è stata   20 ha tradotto

Exercise 4

1 Abbiamo già fatto questo esercizio.   2 Non ho ancora finito di leggere il
giornale.   3 Stefano non è mai andato *or* stato a Roma.   4 Non ho più visto
Roberto, dopo la festa.   5 Avete già pagato il conto?   6 Giulia non ha
ancora cominciato a lavorare.   7 Carlo non ha più potuto lavorare.   8 Non
ho mai conosciuto i suoi genitori.   9 Hai già scritto le lettere?   10 Non ho
mai visto quel film.

UNIT 13

Exercise 1

1 li ho messi   2 l'ho accompagnata   3 le ho comprate   4 le ha chiuse   5 li ho mangiati   6 ti ha chiamata   7 l'ha letto   8 ci hanno invitati   9 li ho presi   10 li ho dati

Exercise 2

1 le ho offerto   2 li avete visti   3 l'ho imprestata   4 le ho telefonato   5 le ha prese   6 li ho studiati   7 mi ha presentato   8 ti ha accompagnata   9 le hai mandato   10 l'ho conosciuta   11 l'abbiamo lasciata   12 gli hai detto   13 li ho comprati   14 L'ho trovata   15 le ho conosciute   16 gli ho detto   17 l'ha pagato   18 le ho raccontato   19 L'ha accompagnata   20 l'ho letta tutta

Exercise 3

1 Non li ho saputi fare.   2 Li ho voluti vedere.   3 Non l'abbiamo potuto chiamare.   4 Vi hanno potuti aiutare *or* potute aiutare?   5 L'abbiamo dovuta invitare.   6 Non le ha sapute tradurre.   7 Le avete dovute accompagnare?   8 L'ha voluta mangiare.   9 Li hai potuti vedere?   10 Non le hanno volute fare.

Exercise 4

1 Sabina non mi ha invitata.   2 Chi ti ha chiamata?   3 Gli abbiamo telefonato ieri.   4 Vi ho cercati, ma non vi ho trovati.   5 Chiara ci ha accompagnati *or* portati alla fermata dell'autobus.   6 Vi ho mandato una cartolina, l'avete ricevuta?   7 I (miei) nonni mi hanno regalato 100 euro, ma li ho già spesi.   8 Ho comprato due panini e li ho mangiati.   9 'Hai spento la luce?' 'Sì, l'ho spenta.'   10 Carla non ha potuto aiutarle *or* Carla non le ha potute aiutare.

UNIT 14

Exercise 1

1 lei, te   2 loro   3 lei   4 noi, voi   5 me   6 lui   7 me, te   8 Lei   9 voi   10 lei, loro

Exercise 2

1 Nobody plays drums like <u>me</u>.   2 Every student but him did the homework.   3 Sergio calls *or* phones <u>you</u>, not me.   4 I'll take *or* go with *or*

accompany <u>you</u> as well.   5 I understand as much as you do *or* as much as <u>you</u>.   6 Mauro tells everyone the truth but *or* except me.   7 You should *or* you must *or* you have to phone <u>me</u> as well.   8 Claudia's lending <u>us</u> the records, not <u>you</u>.   9 I'm giving *or* I give *or* I'll give my address to everyone but her.   10 I'm giving <u>her</u> a book and <u>him</u> a record.

Exercise 3

1 voi   2 lui   3 loro   4 noi   5 lei

Exercise 4

1 Tutti sono contro di me!   2 Vieni con me?   3 Ho comprato un regalo per te.   4 Non puoi contare su di lui.   5 Posso dormire da voi, stasera?

UNIT 15

Exercise 1

1 che   2 cui   3 che   4 cui   5 che   6 che   7 cui   8 cui   9 cui   10 che

Exercise 2

1 cui   2 cui   3 cui   4 che   5 che   6 che   7 cui   8 che   9 cui   10 cui

Exercise 3

1 la quale   2 con la quale   3 dei quali   4 nel quale   5 alle quali   6 il quale   7 dal quale   8 le quali   9 delle quali   10 i quali

Exercise 4

1 colei che   2 coloro che   3 colui che   4 colui *or* colei che   5 coloro che

Exercise 5

1 chi   2 quella che   3 chi *or* quello che   4 chi   5 quelli che   6 quella che   7 chi 8 quello che   9 chi   10 quelle che

Exercise 6

1 Il libro che voglio comprare è troppo caro.   2 La signora con cui *or* con la quale ho parlato è tedesca.   3 Le persone che *or* le quali hanno telefonato vivono *or* abitano in America!   4 La città dove *or* in cui *or* nella quale vivo *or*

abito non è molto grande.   5 Colui che *or* chi vuole andare all'università deve sapere leggere e scrivere.   6 Paolo, che *or* il quale ha perso il (suo) cellulare, non è contento *or* felice.   7 Quella canzone mi piace *or* Mi piace quella canzone, ma preferisco quelle che abbiamo sentito ieri sera.   8 Questa è *or* Ecco la sorella di Fabio, la quale *or* che mi ha prestato la sua bici.   9 Hai visto chi *or* colui che *or* colei che ha mangiato le pesche?   10 Chi è l'uomo cui *or* a cui *or* al quale avete venduto i biglietti?

UNIT 16

Exercise 1

1 parlava   2 passava   3 faceva   4 studiavo, riposava   5 partiva   6 lavorava   7 diceva   8 faceva   9 abitavamo   10 eravate   11 andavano   12 era   13 uscivamo   14 sapevi   15 conoscevo   16 amava   17 dormivate   18 erano   19 avevi   20 dovevano

Exercise 2

1 sei partita   2 era   3 ho studiato   4 mangiavamo   5 è rimasta   6 aveva   7 sembravano   8 ha speso   9 è andata   10 erano

Exercise 3

1 è arrivato, era   2 ho conosciuto, abitavo   3 avevi, hai cominciato   4 ha telefonato, facevo   5 sono venuti, era   6 hanno fatto, sapevano   7 hanno detto, hanno visto   8 è venuto, aveva   9 siamo arrivati *or* arrivate, partiva   10 ho imprestato, era

Exercise 4

suonava, piaceva, abbiamo deciso, siamo arrivati, mancavano, c'erano, era, aspettavamo, abbiamo sentito, ha risposto, abbiamo visto, era, ha finito, ha spiegato, era, chiamava, aveva, era, sapeva, è partito, aveva, è riuscito, aprivano

Exercise 5

1 Quanto tempo hai passato a Bologna?   2 Siamo andati *or* andate al cinema ieri sera.   3 Sembravate felici.   4 Il padre di Gemma faceva il marinaio *or* era marinaio.   5 Claudia e Monica non sono venute in vacanza con noi questa volta.   6 I miei genitori di solito uscivano alle 8.   7 Mio padre ha lavorato in India per 3 anni.   8 A che ora avete preso l'autobus ieri mattina?   9 L'anno scorso facevamo ginnastica il *or* di lunedì mattina.   10 Dove hai

comprato quelle scarpe?   11 Non ti ho chiamato *or* chiamata perché dormivi.
12 Quando voi abitavate *or* vivevate a Londra io abitavo *or* vivevo a Parigi.
13 Quanti anni aveva Susanna quando è andata all'università?   14 Mentre
guardavo la televisione, Anna è entrata e l'ha spenta.   15 Paolo e Giulia non
sono venuti perché Paolo era troppo stanco.

UNIT 17

Exercise 1

1 ne ho mandate   2 ne ho comprata *or* ne ho comprati   3 ne ho fatti *or* ne ho
fatta   4 ne sono venute poche   5 non ne ho fatto nessuno   6 ne ho lasciata
una aperta   7 ne hanno invitati molti   8 ne ho letti   9 ne abbiamo comprata poca   10 non ne ho mangiata nessuna   11 ne ho presi   12 ne ho date
alcune   13 ne abbiamo visti   14 ne ho mangiate   15 non ne ha mangiato
nessuno   16 ne abbiamo dato qualcuno   17 ne ho presi alcuni   18 ne sono
rimasti, alcuni, cari   19 non ne ha invitata nessuna   20 ne ho regalate

Exercise 2

1 ne   2 ne   3 li   4 l'   5 ne   6 le   7 ne   8 ne   9 li   10 ne   11 ne   12 l'
13 ne   14 ne   15 ne   16 la   17 lo   18 ne   19 ne   20 li

Exercise 3

1 Dovete parlarne col professore.   2 Vuoi farne un altro?   3 Non dobbiamo
prenderne.   4 Potete mangiarne.   5 Devo farne sei.   6 Non possiamo parlarne.   7 Posso assaggiarne uno?   8 Non deve portarne, Signora.   9 Vogliono comprarne qualcuno.   10 Non possono berne.

Exercise 4

1 Ne ho dovuti dare due a Marisa.   2 Ne hai potute comprare?   3 Quante
ne hai dovute fare?   4 Non ne hanno voluta mangiare.   5 Ne ha dovuti
leggere quattro.   6 Non ne abbiamo potute prendere.   7 Ne ho dovute scrivere due.   8 Ne ho potute leggere solo due pagine.   9 Ne avete dovuti rifare
molti?   10 Non ne hanno potuta assaggiare.

Exercise 5

1 in questa casa; Ci abitiamo da tre anni.   2 al Museo di Storia Naturale;
Stefano ci lavora da febbraio.   3 alla festa di Marco; Ci volete venire? *or*
Volete venirci?   4 al cinema; Paolo e Livia ci vanno due volte alla set-
timana.   5 al supermercato; La Signora Bini ci va sempre a piedi.   6 in

Italia; Ci rimango per tre settimane. 7 a scuola; Giulia ci viene sempre in bici. 8 all'ufficio postale; Ci ho passato tre ore in coda. 9 a casa di Pietro; Ci siete andati a cena? 10 a Sorrento; Ci passiamo le vacanze.

UNIT 18

Exercise 1

1 arriveranno 2 parlerete 3 telefonerà 4 dirai 5 scriverò 6 dormirò 7 cominceremo 8 finirai 9 prenderò 10 chiamerai 11 abiterete 12 porteranno 13 direte 14 tradurrà 15 pagheremo 16 mangerai 17 scriverà 18 cercherà 19 prenderanno 20 pagherà

Exercise 2

1 andrò 2 saremo 3 rimarrai 4 verrò, potrò 5 dovrà 6 verrà, vorrà 7 avremo 8 potrò 9 vedrai 10 farete 11 staranno 12 saprà 13 farai 14 sarete 15 dovrete 16 andrò 17 saprai 18 verrai 19 farete 20 terranno

Exercise 3

uscirò, dovrò, arriverò, verrà, andremo, lascerò, andremo, vedremo, porterà, torneremo, verranno, dovremo, usciremo, faremo, sarà, potremo

Exercise 4

1 Chi potrà aiutarmi? 2 L'estate prossima faremo un corso di italiano. 3 Leggerai tutti questi libri? 4 Non andrò in biblioteca domani. 5 Quando arriverà, Signora Pasini? 6 Domenica usciranno. 7 Cosa farai? 8 Saranno le 10. 9 Porterai i tuoi CD per la festa? 10 Non verrete con noi al cinema?

UNIT 19

Exercise 1

1 aveva finito 2 era arrivata 3 avevo vista 4 avevi spento 5 avevate preso 6 aveva lavorato 7 aveva scritto 8 aveva preparato 9 eri riuscito *or* riuscita 10 avevamo chiesto 11 era stata 12 avevo mangiato 13 era piaciuta 14 era andata 15 erano uscite 16 avevo capito 17 era partito 18 era rimasto 19 aveva voluto 20 era stata

Exercise 2

1 sono arrivato *or* arrivata, erano usciti   2 conosceva, aveva telefonato.
3 hai fatto, avevo detto   4 era, aveva camminato   5 è venuto, doveva *or* ha
dovuto, avevano dato   6 era, aveva vinto   7 portava, aveva regalato   8 ho
comprato, avevate consigliato   9 ha speso, aveva guadagnato   10 ha invitato, erano andati

Exercise 3

1 Paola non era ancora andata *or* stata in Scozia.   2 Avevo finito il lavoro,
ma ero molto stanco *or* stanca.   3 Le ragazze non erano mai entrate in quella
chiesa.   4 Arianna ha finito la torta che aveva fatto sua nonna.   5 'Cosa
avevi detto a Fabio?' 'Non gli avevo detto nulla.'   6 Maria aveva dovuto *or*
era dovuta rimanere *or* restare a casa.   7 Quanto era costata la vostra
macchina *or* auto?   8 Avevano comprato *or* preso il biglietto il giorno
prima.   9 Non avevo più la bici, perché l'avevo data a Anna.   10 Era nata in
Russia, ma abitava da molti anni in Italia quando l'ho conosciuta.

UNIT 20

Exercise 1

1 si   2 mi   3 si   4 vi   5 si   6 ci   7 mi   8 si   9 si   10 si   11 vi   12 ti
13 ci   14 si   15 vi   16 si   17 si   18 ti   19 vi   20 si

Exercise 2

1 si   2 si   3 vi   4 si   5 ti   6 ci   7 si   8 si   9 ci   10 mi   11 vi   12 ci
13 si   14 ti   15 mi   16 ti   17 ci   18 si   19 mi   20 vi

Exercise 3

1 si sono sposati   2 ti sei sbagliato   3 vi siete ricordate   4 si è fatta   5 si
sono incontrati   6 ti sei perso   7 si è divertita   8 ci siamo bevuti   9 mi sono
annoiato   10 ci siamo alzate   11 ti sei lavato   12 mi sono tagliata   13 si è
fermato   14 si sono separati   15 si è lamentato   16 si è riposato   17 si è
stancata   18 ti sei arrabbiata   19 vi siete offesi   20 si sono dimenticati

Exercise 4

1 Non mi sono potuta lavare.   2 Sandra e Roberto si sono voluti sposare.
3 Ci siamo dovuti scusare.   4 Luigi si è dovuto alzare alle sei.   5 Gianni non
si è voluto mettere il berretto.   6 Ti sei potuto curare?   7 Vi siete potuti

riposare?   8 Mi sono dovuta fermare.   9 Perché ti sei voluto tingere i capelli?   10 Non ci siamo potuti spiegare.

Exercise 5

1 Vi divertite?   2 Ti sei lavata le mani?   3 Come si sente, Signora?   4 Vi sbagliate.   5 Dove vi siete conosciute *or* incontrate?   6 Perché non ti siedi?   7 Paolo parla sempre di sè *or* se stesso.   8 Franca si è lavata i capelli.   9 Carlo si è scusato.   10 Mi sono vestita.

UNIT 21

Exercise 1

1 compra   2 usciamo   3 stia   4 metti   5 siate   6 venga   7 dai *or* da'   8 finisci   9 compri   10 facciamo   11 abbi   12 parli   13 vai *or* va'   14 di'   15 faccia   16 scrivete   17 fai *or* fa'   18 entrino   19 aprite   20 rispondi

Exercise 2

1 chiuda   2 vada   3 sorrida   4 dica   5 faccia   6 sia   7 traduca   8 accenda   9 stia   10 entri

Exercise 3

1 non partite   2 non rispondere   3 non andate   4 non scenda   5 non usciamo   6 non finire   7 non ascoltare   8 non prenda   9 non telefonare   10 non dire   11 non tagliarti *or* non ti tagliare   12 non darle *or* non le dare   13 non parlargli *or* non gli parlare   14 non scrivetemi *or* non mi scrivete   15 non dirlo *or* non lo dire   16 non invitarli *or* non li invitare   17 non prenderlo *or* non lo prendere   18 non metterti *or* non ti mettere   19 non portatele *or* non le portate   20 non farlo *or* non lo fare

Exercise 4

1 vai *or* va'   2 prendete   3 invita   4 guardiamo   5 comincia   6 faccia   7 mettano   8 fai *or* fa'   9 vai *or* va'   10 stai *or* sta'   11 mandami   12 fatelo   13 dammi   14 rispondimi   15 vacci   16 mangiatelo   17 leggetelo   18 ci aspetti   19 digli   20 dalle

Exercise 5

1 parlatele   2 prendili   3 lo firmi   4 parlatene   5 andiamoci   6 falli   7 restateci   8 chiediamolo   9 correggili   10 prendetelo   11 lo aspettino

12 mandali   13 compratela   14 la porti   15 aiutateli   16 rendilo   17 chiediamole   18 telefonagli *or* telefona loro   19 bevine   20 studiatela

UNIT 22

Exercise 1

1 fa, attraversa   2 parlano   3 lavora   4 fuma   5 devono   6 entra   7 possono   8 paga   9 trovano   10 compra

Exercise 2

1 Quando si ha freddo, si lavora male.   2 Quando si ha la febbre, si resta a casa.   3 Quando si comincia a studiare una lingua, si fanno degli sbagli. 4 Quando si guida non si usa il cellulare.   5 Quando si ha fame si mangia. 6 Quando si è stanchi si fanno molti sbagli.   7 Quando si è avvocati si conosce la legge.   8 Quando non si hanno soldi, non si fanno spese inutili. 9 Quando si hanno tanti amici si è fortunati.   10 Quando si mangiano troppi dolci, si ingrassa.

Exercise 3

1 Non si mettono i piedi sulla scrivania.   2 La mattina si fa colazione. 3 Dopo pranzo si lavano i piatti.   4 Non si parla con gli sconosciuti.   5 Non si va in bicicletta sul marciapiedi.   6 Non si mangia durante le lezioni. 7 Non ci si guarda tanto allo specchio.   8 In biblioteca si parla a bassa voce.   9 Non si guarda la televisione tutto il giorno.   10 Il giorno prima degli esami si studia.

Exercise 4

1 Dopo che si è fatto il bagno in mare, si fa la doccia.   2 Dopo che si è superato un esame, si è contenti.   3 Dopo che si è finito di lavorare si va a casa.   4 Dopo che si è saliti sull'aereo, non si può usare il cellulare. 5 Quando si è cresciuti in campagna, si conoscono i nomi di tante piante.

UNIT 23

Exercise 1

1 leggeresti   2 potrei   3 avreste   4 sveglieresti   5 vorrebbero   6 paghe-resti   7 farei   8 dovremmo   9 sapresti   10 rimarrebbe   11 aprirei 12 dovresti   13 piacerebbe   14 potrebbe   15 sarebbe   16 dareste   17 berrei   18 abiterebbero   19 tradurrebbe   20 accompagneresti

Exercise 2

1 Vorrei due panini.   2 Dovreste studiare di più.   3 Lucia andrebbe in vacanza.   4 Fareste una pausa?   5 Potremmo parlarti?   6 Maurizio cambierebbe lavoro.   7 Mi daresti un consiglio?   8 Vi piacerebbe andare a Venezia?   9 I nostri amici dovrebbero arrivare oggi.   10 Non uscirebbe mai senza permesso.

Exercise 3

1 Paola potrebbe aiutarmi *or* mi potrebbe aiutare.   2 Verremmo volentieri.   3 Non andrei in biblioteca la *or* di sera.   4 Quando comincerebbe, Signora Vialli?   5 Pietro vorrebbe invitarti *or* ti vorrebbe invitare alla festa.   6 Saremmo contenti *or* felici di vedervi.   7 Terrebbero il cane in giardino.   8 Dovrei partire presto.   9 Vorrei un altro biscotto.   10 Saprebbe il risultato, Signor Spadavecchia?

GLOSSARY OF TECHNICAL TERMS

adjective   a word that describes a noun or pronoun, e.g. the *green* door; it's very *old*; John's *skinny*; she's most *objectionable*:

a **demonstrative adjective** describes something as being pointed out ('demonstrated'), e.g. *this/that* computer; *these/those* railings;

a **possessive adjective** describes something as belonging to someone or something, e.g. *my/her/its/our/your* behaviour is quite normal.

adverb   a word which gives information about a verb, an adjective or another adverb, e.g. she sang *loudly*; it'll finish *soon*; I've got it *somewhere*; it's *incredibly/very* funny; she sang *incredibly/very loudly*.

agreement   a feature whereby the form of one word changes depending on the form of another word it is linked with. In English, the most obvious example is in the difference between singular and plural: so we say '*This is* the *road*' and '*These are* the *roads*', but not e.g. '*This are* the roads', '*These is* the roads', etc. In Italian, agreement is far more detailed and widespread than in English.

article   a word which has no meaning on its own, but is placed before a noun to show whether it is specific or non-specific:

a **definite article** shows that the noun refers to a specific thing or person, e.g. *the* airline; *the* pilot; *the* passengers;

an **indefinite article** shows that the noun does not refer to a specific thing or person, e.g. *an* airline; *a* pilot; passengers [no plural indefinite article].

auxiliary verb   a verb that helps another verb to make its form, e.g. we *have* done it; it *had* been agreed.

conjugation   a group of verbs which have the same endings as one another in all tenses; e.g. in Italian, verbs of the first conjugation have an infinitive ending in -*are* (compr*are*, 'to buy', cant*are*, 'to sing') and the same endings in the present (compr*ano*, 'they buy', cant*ano*, 'they sing'), the imperfect (compr*avano*, 'they bought', cant*avano*, 'they sang'), the future (compre-*ranno*, 'they will buy', cant*eranno*, 'they will sing'), etc.

gender   not the same thing as the actual sex of a living creature, grammatical gender is arbitrary; in Italian, all nouns are either masculine or feminine, even if they denote inanimate objects, e.g. il libro [m], 'the book', la casa [f], 'the house', etc.

infinitive   the form in which verbs are usually given in word lists etc., e.g. vendere, 'to sell', dormire, 'to sleep'.

noun   the name of a thing, person, place, animal, plant, idea, e.g. the green *door*; *John* is skinny; *love* is a wonderful *thing*; I love *cats* and *roses*.

number   a feature of nouns, pronouns and any words that agree with them (notably, in Italian, adjectives, articles and verbs) which shows whether there is just one, or more than one, of the thing or person in question. If there is one, then the noun, pronoun, etc. is **singular**, e.g. the *mobile*; a *child*; *I/she/he/it*; if there is more than one, then the noun, pronoun, etc. is **plural**, e.g. the *mobiles*; the *children*; *we/they*. In Italian, the form of the word usually makes it clear whether it is singular or plural, but in English it is often impossible to tell from the word on its own, e.g. one *sheep*; fifty *sheep*; Jim, *you are brilliant*; *you are* all *brilliant*.

object   the noun or pronoun affected by the action of the verb:

a **direct object** is directly impinged on by the action, e.g. I sent *a letter*; the dog drank *its water*; you've shut *the door*; she cooked *it*; I love *him*;

an **indirect object** is the thing/person to or for which/whom the action is performed, e.g. I sent a letter to *Jim*; I gave *her* a CD [i.e. a CD to her]; he built a snowman for *Catherine*; I made *her* a puppet [i.e. a puppet for her].

participle   a form of the verb that 'participates' in characteristics of both verb and adjective, i.e. it both indicates an action and describes something:

the **present participle** in English ends in -*ing*, and is used descriptively even with verbs in a past tense, e.g. she's *running*; Wayne was *shouting*;

the **past participle** in English (as in Italian) is mostly used to form the present perfect tense, e.g. the frog has *jumped* in; she's *run* away; it can also be used purely as an adjective, e.g. it's small but perfectly *formed*; that's a *torn* handkerchief.

passive   a passive verb is the opposite to an active one. Here is an active verb: 'Kylie *drew* that cartoon'; in this sentence, the thing that has something done to it (the cartoon) is the object of the active verb. Now here is the same idea expressed with a passive verb: 'That cartoon *was drawn* by Kylie'; in this sentence, the thing that has something done to it is actually the subject of the passive verb. Many ideas can be expressed both actively and passively, e.g.

Active	Passive
Jim *clapped* Tony [object] on the back.	Tony [subject] *was clapped* on the back by Jim.
She alone *dismissed* the idea [object].	The idea [subject] *was dismissed* by her alone.
They *sell* wild mushrooms [object] here.	Wild mushrooms [subject] *are sold* here (by them).

preposition   a word usually placed in front of a noun or pronoun to show the relation between it and another noun or pronoun, e.g. the cat sat *on* the mat; I've shown them *to* him; the door's *opposite* the bus stop, you just go *through* it.

pronoun   a word that stands for ('pro') a noun:

demonstrative pronouns   stand for particular people or things that are 'pointed to', e.g. *this/that* [i.e. 'this one/that one'] is a dandelion; *these/those* are filthy;

interrogative pronouns   stand for people or things about which a question is being asked, e.g. *what* are you doing? *which* of them did best? *who* won? *who(m)* did you vote for?;

personal pronouns   usually stand for people, e.g. *she* lost her mobile; *they* are happy; *we* phoned *them*; *you* gave *us* a fright;

possessive pronouns   stand for things mentioned as belonging to someone, e.g. this tuna sandwich is *mine* [i.e. 'my one']; those are *yours/hers/theirs*, etc.;

reciprocal pronouns   stand for two or more people or things which reciprocate an action, e.g. they like *each other/one another*; we all gave *each other/one another* birthday presents;

reflexive pronouns   stand for people or things that are both the subject and the object of the verb, e.g. you're wearing *yourselves* out; the dog'll scratch *itself*; the computer switched *itself* off; she bought *herself* something nice;

relative pronouns   usually stand for people or things already mentioned, e.g. the idiot *who* conceded the penalty; the DVDs *which/that* were on the table; the one politician *whom* everyone trusts.

subject   the noun or pronoun that performs the action of the verb, e.g. *Mick* sang solo; *the grass* is green; *you* have grown; *they* say *it* will be easy; *the allegation* was denied; *he* was tripped over.

tense   the form of a verb that corresponds to a particular segment of time, e.g. I *eat* [present]; I *shall eat* [future]; I *have eaten* [present perfect]; I *ate* [simple past]; I *was eating* [past progressive]; I *had eaten* [past perfect].

verb   the word that indicates the performance of an action or the existence of a state, e.g. she *jumped* out of her skin; I *shall get* a mobile; that *is* nice; they *have been* very happy.

INDEX